# The Odd Women

A play by Michael Meyer
After the novel by George Gissing

Samuel French - London
New York - Toronto - Hollywood

© 1993 by MICHAEL MEYER

Rights of Performance by Amateurs are controlled by Samuel French Ltd, 52 Fitzroy Street, London W1P 6JR, and they, or their authorized agents, issue licences to amateurs on payment of a fee. **It is an infringement of the Copyright to give any performance or public reading of the play before the fee has been paid and the licence issued.**

The Royalty Fee indicated below is subject to contract and subject to variation at the sole discretion of Samuel French Ltd.

> Basic fee for each and every
> performance by amateurs        Code M
> in the British Isles

The Professional Rights in this play are controlled by CASAROTTO RAMSAY LTD, National House, 60–66 Wardour Street, London W1V 3HP.

---

The publication of this play does not imply that it is necessarily available for performance by amateurs or professionals, either in the British Isles or Overseas. Amateurs and professionals considering a production are strongly advised in their own interests to apply to the appropriate agents for consent before starting rehearsals or booking a theatre or hall.

---

ISBN 0 573 01852 9

Please see page iv for further copyright information

NL000 10613

| NORFOLK LIBRARY AND INFORMATION SERVICE | |
|---|---|
| SUPPLIER | french |
| INVOICE No. | 13034 |
| ORDER DATE | 28.7.94 |
| COPY No. | |

# CHARACTERS

**Monica Madden**
**Edmund Widdowson**
**Mary Barfoot**
**Bella Royston**
**Rhoda Nunn**
**Alice Madden**
**Virginia Madden**
**Everard Barfoot**
**Alfred,** a manservant
**Harry Bevis**

The action takes place in London and the Lake District in 1888–89

## COPYRIGHT INFORMATION

(See also page ii)

This play is fully protected under the Copyright Laws of the British Commonwealth of Nations, the United States of America and all countries of the Berne and Universal Copyright Conventions.

All rights including Stage, Motion Picture, Radio, Television, Public Reading, and Translation into Foreign Languages, are strictly reserved.

**No part of this publication may lawfully be reproduced in ANY form or by any means—photocopying, typescript, recording (including video-recording), manuscript, electronic, mechanical, or otherwise—or be transmitted or stored in a retrieval system, without prior permission.**

Licences for amateur performances are issued subject to the understanding that it shall be made clear in all advertising matter that the audience will witness an amateur performance; that the names of the authors of the plays shall be included on all programmes; and that the integrity of the authors' work will be preserved.

The Royalty Fee is subject to contract and subject to variation at the sole discretion of Samuel French Ltd.

In Theatres or Halls seating Four Hundred or more the fee will be subject to negotiation.

In Territories Overseas the fee quoted above may not apply. A fee will be quoted on application to our local authorized agent, or if there is no such agent, on application to Samuel French Ltd, London.

### VIDEO RECORDING OF AMATEUR PRODUCTIONS

Please note that the copyright laws governing video-recording are extremely complex and that it should not be assumed that any play may be video-recorded for whatever purpose without first obtaining the permission of the appropriate agents. The fact that a play is published by Samuel French Ltd does not indicate that video rights are available or that Samuel French Ltd controls such rights.

## THE ODD WOMEN

This dramatization was commissioned by the Royal Exchange Theatre, Manchester, and was first performed there on 19th November 1992 with the following cast:

| | |
|---|---|
| **Monica Madden** | Lucy Scott |
| **Edmund Widdowson** | Sean Arnold |
| **Mary Barfoot** | Sorcha Cusack |
| **Bella Royston** | Michelle Chadwick |
| **Rhoda Nunn** | Lorraine Ashbourne |
| **Alice Madden** | Susan Tordoff |
| **Virginia Madden** | Tilly Tremayne |
| **Everard Barfoot** | Paul Higgins |
| **Alfred** | Alan Pattison |
| **Harry Bevis** | John Skitt |

Directed by Braham Murray
Designed by Johanna Bryant

## SYNOPSIS OF SCENES

### ACT I
SCENE 1  By the Thames in Battersea Park. Summer 1888
SCENE 2  Mary Barfoot's house in Chelsea
SCENE 3  Battersea Park
SCENE 4  Mary's house in Chelsea
SCENE 5  Battersea Park
SCENE 6  Mary's house in Chelsea
SCENE 7  Alice's and Virginia's room
SCENE 8  Chelsea Gardens
SCENE 9  Widdowson's house

### ACT II
SCENE 1  The Royal Academy
SCENE 2  Widdowson's house
SCENE 3  Mary's house in Chelsea
SCENE 4  Bevis's flat
SCENE 5  Widdowson's house
SCENE 6  The Lake District
SCENE 7  Bevis's flat
SCENE 8  Mary's house in Chelsea
SCENE 9  The Lake District
SCENE 10  Mary's house in Chelsea
SCENE 11  Widdowson's house
SCENE 12  Mary's house in Chelsea. Some months later
SCENE 13  The same

# George Gissing

George Gissing was born in Wakefield, Yorkshire on 22nd November 1857, the son of a pharmacist. A brilliant classics and language student, he won prizes for Greek, Latin, German, English and Poetry at Owens College, Manchester, boarding for his first two years at Alderley Edge.

In his third year, just turned eighteen, he moved into Manchester, where he became infatuated with a prostitute named Nell Harrison whom he had picked up in a pub. In an effort to get her to give up her trade he gave her all his money, even selling his watch, and finally in desperation stole from his fellow students' lockers. For this he was expelled and sentenced to a month's hard labour. On leaving prison he sailed, in September 1876, to America, taught for some months at a school near Boston, then moved to Chicago, where he published his first fiction, some twenty short stories, in various local papers. In September 1877 he returned to England and settled in London, determined to keep himself by writing. Nell joined him. He wrote a novel which was rejected and which he destroyed, then another, *Workers in the Dawn*, about a man who tries unsuccessfully to save a prostitute by marrying her. Over 1,200 pages long, it was rejected by various publishers, and Gissing brought it out at his own expense, using part of the few hundred pounds which he had received from a great-aunt's estate on attaining his majority. It was little noticed but found a few admirers. Four years later, in 1884, there appeared his second novel, *The Unclassed*, also about a man who marries a prostitute. Between 1885 and 1895, he published fourteen novels, including some of his finest—*Demos*, about early socialism, *The Nether World*, about life among the London poor, *New Grub Street*, about a writer whose early success is followed by creative impotence and the break-up of his marriage, *The Odd Women* and *In the Year of Jubilee*. But although he was by now one of the four most esteemed living British novelists, with Hardy, Stevenson and Meredith, his books never sold really well and he remained poor. Even after he and Nell parted in 1882 (she died of drink, syphilis, cold and hunger in 1888), he bewailed that he could never invite any woman of his own social class out because his lodgings and clothes were so wretched and he could not afford a restaurant or a decent spare suit.

In 1890 he made an equally disastrous second marriage with Edith Underwood, the daughter of a monumental mason whom he picked up at a tea garden in Kew. "He was very hard up and hopelessly and fearfully oppressed by sex necessity", wrote his friend, H G Wells. "I believe he was too poor for prostitutes . . . He felt that to make love to any woman he could regard as a social equal would be too elaborate, restrained and tedious for his urgencies . . . so for the second time he flung himself at a social inferior whom he expected to be easy and grateful . . . Never did a man need mothering more, and never was there a less sacrificial lover." Gissing's most recent biographer, John Halperin, suggests that in marrying so obviously unsuitable a wife (Edith was also mentally unstable and in 1902 was committed to an asylum, where she died in 1917), Gissing "was still punishing himself for his past crimes, performing an act of aggressive, irrational 'respectability' to make up for previous irregularities". Halperin suggests that Gissing "considered misery a necessary ingredient of his art. If it was misery he was after, he was to find more that he bargained for in his second marriage. It is not wholly accidental, then, that many of his best novels were written in the nineties".

Edith bore him two sons, the elder of whom was killed on the Somme, the younger dying as recently as 1975. She and Gissing separated in 1897. The following summer a twenty-nine-year-old Frenchwoman, Gabrielle Fleury, wrote to him asking if she might translate *New Grub Street*. They met, fell in love and settled down together in France. Gissing seems to have found at least a measure of happiness in this relationship, which lasted until his death of pneumonia and attendant complications at Ispoure, near St Jean Pied de Port in South West France, on 28th December 1903, aged forty-six.

Although Gissing has never been a popular author, he has always been admired by fellow writers, from Woolf and Wells to Greene and Orwell. "I am ready to maintain that England has produced very few better novelists", wrote Orwell in 1948. "I think *The Odd Women* is one of the best novels in English."

Michael Meyer

For Braham and Johanna
with love and thanks

# ACT I

### Scene 1

*By the Thames in Battersea Park. The summer of 1888. Monica Madden, a pretty girl of twenty, simply dressed, is seated on a bench reading a library book. From a short distance Edmund Widdowson watches her. He is forty-four, with greying hair and beard, well-dressed, upright and strongly built, but seems diffident*

**Widdowson** Would you mind if I sat here?

*She nods. He sits at the other end of the bench and opens a book. For a short while they read in silence. At length Widdowson looks towards her*

  May I ask what you are reading?
**Monica** (*embarrassed at being thus accosted, hesitates*) "The Mayor of Casterbridge".
**Widdowson** (*approvingly*) Ah. You admire Thomas Hardy?
**Monica** Very much.
**Widdowson** So do I. I do not understand how some critics can accuse him of being immoral.
**Monica** Do they?
**Widdowson** Indeed, yes. I find him the most moral of writers. In addition to being a profound student of human character.
**Monica** And of the soul.
**Widdowson** And of the soul. And he understands women so well. If one compares him with Dickens, for instance. I presume you have read Dickens?
**Monica** Not yet. I have so little time for reading. Only Sundays really.
**Widdowson** Why is that?
**Monica** I work in a shop, and the hours are very long.
**Widdowson** I am sorry to hear that. (*Pause*) Forgive my saying, but you look, and sound, too genteel a young lady to work in a shop. Unless of course it belongs to your family. I am sorry, I should have guessed that.
**Monica** No, I work at Scotcher's in Wandsworth. Perhaps you know it? A big department store.
**Widdowson** (*surprised*) I have heard of it. I do not live in this area. I live in Herne Hill.
**Monica** That is a long way from here. Did you come by train?
**Widdowson** No, in my trap. I thought I would rest my horse and take a stroll by the river. I hope you do not think it forward of me to have engaged you in conversation. I live alone, and sometimes do not speak to anyone for several days except my housekeeper.
**Monica** Surely you meet people at your work?
**Widdowson** I only work two days a week. That surprises you? (*He laughs*)

Last year my only brother died. Unlike me, he had been successful in business and left me what I regard as a small fortune, though it was only a fraction of his wealth. I decided to semi-retire and read all the books I had no time to read when I was young. Reading is my life.

**Monica** (*looks at her watch*) I am afraid I must be going.

**Widdowson** (*rises courteously*) I have enjoyed our conversation. (*He offers his hand*)

**Monica** (*accepts it*) So have I.

**Widdowson** (*after a moment*) We meet in this casual way and talk, and then say goodbye. If you were a man I would give you my card and invite you to my house. The card at least I may offer. (*He takes out a card case and extracts a card which he gives her*) My name, as you see, is Edmund Widdowson.

**Monica** (*without looking at it*) Thank you.

**Widdowson** I should like if possible to continue this conversation. Could I perhaps meet you here next Sunday? I take it you are only free on Sundays?

**Monica** (*long pause*) Very well. But if it is raining——?

**Widdowson** Then the Sunday after. (*He laughs*) The first Sunday when it does not rain. At this time,

**Monica** Very well.

*Monica goes*

**Widdowson** (*softly*) What is your name?

*But she does not hear him*

## SCENE 2

*Mary Barfoot's house in Chelsea*

*It is elegant and comfortable without ostentation*

*Mary, forty-three, is seated at a primitive typewriter. We hear her clatter at the keys for a few seconds before the Lights go up. The doorbell rings. Mary goes to open it*

*Bella Royston is there. She is twenty-two, pretty but poorly dressed*

**Bella** (*nervously*) Miss Barfoot?

**Mary** (*unwelcoming*) Bella. I am surprised to see you.

**Bella** Please may I speak with you for a few minutes?

*Pause*

**Mary** Is there any point?

**Bella** Please.

**Mary** Very well. (*She does not invite her to sit*) What have you to say to me? I am expecting guests.

**Bella** I have come to ask if you will take me back.

## Act I, Scene 2

**Mary** You know the principles on which my school is run.
**Bella** (*meekly*) Yes.
**Mary** Miss Nunn and I founded it to train young women to earn their own living. Instead of just waiting for a husband.
**Bella** I know.
**Mary** Yet you chose to give it up to go and live with a married man.
**Bella** I fell in love with him. Was that so wrong?
**Mary** I do not say it was wrong. But you must admit it set a poor example for your fellow pupils.
**Bella** He said he wanted to marry me. I wanted a home of my own, and children. What we all want.
**Mary** Not all.
**Bella** Have you taken a vote on it?
**Mary** You say he wanted to marry you? Did he not foresee the difficulty of obtaining a divorce? Or has his passion cooled?
**Bella** He has left me.
**Mary** Ah. (*Gently*) I am sorry.
**Bella** He promised me so much. Was I foolish to believe him?
**Mary** Yes. Well, perhaps not altogether.
**Bella** I beg you to give me another chance.
**Mary** I must think it over. I will speak with Miss Nunn.
**Bella** I don't think Miss Nunn will forgive me. She is so stern and unbending. Oh, please try to persuade her. Surely I may be forgiven one mistake?
**Mary** Leave me your address. I will write to you.
**Bella** Thank you.

*Mary hands her a piece of paper from the table. Bella writes on it. She kisses Mary's hand. Mary withdraws it*

*Bella leaves*

*Mary returns to the typewriter*

> *After some moments, Rhoda Nunn enters from another room. She is in her thirties, handsome in a forbidding way, without make-up, her hair done in a deliberately unappealing style*

**Rhoda** Who was that?
**Mary** Bella Royston.
**Rhoda** I thought we had heard the last of her. What did she want?
**Mary** That man has left her.
**Rhoda** (*laughs*) Serve her right. I suppose she came for money?
**Mary** No. She asks if we will take her back.
**Rhoda** She must be mad.

*Mary is silent*

   You told her so, I trust.
**Mary** I said I would think about it.
**Rhoda** There must be no question of it.
**Mary** The girl is in despair.

**Rhoda** Send her a cheque.
**Mary** I like her.
**Rhoda** I know. But she isn't a suitable companion for the others.
**Mary** She was infatuated with the man. I don't think she has a bad character.
**Rhoda** Mary, she is not a child. She is twenty-two. She knew the man had a wife. Oh, I admit polygamy is one way of overcoming women's problems. More of them would find comfortable homes, and they would be required to submit less often to their husbands' demands. But I don't imagine it is something that you would advocate.
**Mary** Must one mistake condemn a woman for life? She fell in love.

*Rhoda laughs scornfully*

Have you ever been in love, Rhoda?
**Rhoda** Thank God, no.
**Mary** Then I wonder if you are qualified to judge.
**Rhoda** Mary, you never proposed keeping a reformatory. Our aim is to help young women to be of some use in the world. To readmit Bella would threaten our whole project. Once it became known that you had allowed such a person back, the kind of young women we want would no longer come, and many of those we have would leave. As soon as our moral position comes into question, the school will fold. You must be ruthless in this.
**Mary** Oh, Rhoda. You despise love and the very concept of marriage. Most women would live a wasted life if they did not marry.
**Rhoda** Most women lead a wasted life because they do marry. Don't tell me you regret having remained single.
**Mary** On balance, no.
**Rhoda** On balance?
**Mary** I once loved a man. Or thought I did.
**Rhoda** I didn't know. What happened?
**Mary** Nothing.
**Rhoda** Was that his choice, or yours?
**Mary** Oh, I don't think he noticed me.
**Rhoda** (*glances at her watch*) The Maddens will be here soon. Oh, dear.
**Mary** Why do you say that?
**Rhoda** I gather from their letter that they're having a hard time.
**Mary** Do you know why?
**Rhoda** The usual problem. No husbands and no money. And now no jobs. Well, the youngest is serving in a department store.
**Mary** (*grimaces*) In frightful conditions, no doubt.
**Rhoda** I imagine so. The others have asked if I can help her.

*The doorbell rings*

I'll let them in.

*Rhoda goes to the door and returns with Alice and Virginia Madden. Alice is thirty-five, Virginia thirty-three. Both were once good-looking but have faded through poverty and lack of purpose. They are respectably dressed in clothes that are far from new. Alice is stiff and pedantic, Virginia more graceful in voice and movement*

How nice to see you again. This is my friend, Mary Barfoot. Alice and Virginia Madden.
**Mary** How do you do.
**Virginia** Good-evening.
**Mary** Won't you come and have some tea?
**Rhoda** Is Monica not with you?
**Virginia** She is coming direct from Wandsworth.
**Alice** She lives above the shop.
**Rhoda** Really?
**Virginia** They have a staff dormitory.
**Alice** She has to share with fifteen other girls. So unlike the way our dear father brought us up. She had her own bedroom from the time she was six.
**Rhoda** Yes, I remember you had a large house.
**Virginia** It was very beautiful. We had such a happy childhood, even after dear Mother died. Do you remember the garden?
**Rhoda** Yes. Your father was a wonderful doctor. He saved my life. I shall always be grateful to him.

*Mary pours tea and offers sandwiches. Alice and Virginia bite eagerly into them*

**Alice** I do so miss Somerset. I shall never get used to London. The dirt and the bustle.
**Rhoda** What made you move here?
**Alice** When Father died, he left very little money. (*To Mary*) Most of his patients were poor people. He often didn't charge them anything. Then our little town began to develop as a seaside resort. That would have meant well-to-do patients who could afford to pay. Father had never saved much money because he wanted to give us the best education. He thought he would start saving once we had all left school. But then he was thrown from his horse returning from a patient at night on an icy road, and killed.
**Rhoda** Had he not insured his life?
**Virginia** He talked about doing it. But there didn't seem any urgency. He was only forty-nine and had always been so healthy.
**Mary** Please have another sandwich.
**Alice**
**Virginia** } Thank you.
**Mary** Take two, it will save me asking you again.

*Alice and Virginia glance at each other hesitantly, then do so*

**Rhoda** So what did you do?
**Alice** We tried to get posts as teachers, but had no luck. All the young women of our class want to teach. It is the only thing a respectable woman can do, unless you can afford to keep yourself while training to be a pharmacist, which we couldn't.
**Mary** So?

**Virginia** Alice found a post as a nursery governess, and I became a companion to an elderly lady.
**Rhoda** What did they pay you?
**Alice** Not very generously, I am afraid.
**Rhoda** How much?
**Virginia** Alice got sixteen pounds a year. I had twelve. Of course we had our own room and food.
**Rhoda** But I presume you had to buy your own clothes, so you can't have saved anything.
**Alice** No.
**Rhoda** Tell me more.
**Virginia** Well, Alice's charges went away to school, and my lady died. I had hoped she might leave me a little something in her will, but she never made one, though she talked about it often enough. I don't think she wanted to face the thought of dying.
**Mary** And neither of you has managed to find new employment?
**Alice** You see, we have no degrees or certificates, and without them employers often offer no salary at all, only a room and board.
**Virginia** And we are treated like servants. It is most humiliating. We came to London to be near Monica. Thank heavens we have our faith to comfort us.
**Alice** On Sundays, when it is too cold or rainy to go to church, we read the service aloud in our little room. Of course it is not the same.
**Virginia** We miss the music, which is so beautiful.
**Alice** And the sermon.
**Mary** How much exactly did your father leave?
**Virginia** Eight hundred pounds. The interest brings us an income of thirty-four pounds a year. We give Monica nine pounds a year—it should be more, but as she has a job she can just manage.
**Mary** That leaves twenty-five pounds for the two of you. How can you live on that?
**Virginia** We share a room for seven shillings a week. That leaves seven shillings a week for everything else. But we have learned to eat on sixpence a day.
**Rhoda** What on earth can you get for sixpence?
**Alice** Oh, potatoes and milk, bread, cheese and rice. It is enough. We go to bed early so save lamp oil. As long as we do not fall ill——

*The doorbell rings*

**Mary** That should be Monica. (*She opens the door*)

*Monica is there*

Good-evening. You must be Monica. I am Mary Barfoot.
**Monica** (*nervously*) Good-evening.
**Rhoda** Hallo, Monica.
**Monica** (*pleased*) Rhoda!

*Monica makes to kiss her but Rhoda holds out her hand. Monica takes it*

Act I, Scene 2

Hallo, Alice, Virgie. (*She kisses them*)
**Mary** I'll make some fresh tea.
**Monica** No, please don't bother.
**Mary** Stewed tea is horrible.

*Mary goes out with the pot*

**Rhoda** Well, how long is it since I last saw you? It must be almost ten years.
**Monica** Eleven years, I think.
**Rhoda** So, how is life in a department store?
**Monica** Very tiring.
**Rhoda** I can imagine. Twelve hours a day, isn't it?
**Monica** Thirteen and a half, actually. Monday to Friday——
**Rhoda** Thirteen and a half!
**Monica** You see, the store is open till eight-thirty at night, and it takes another half-hour to tidy up.
**Rhoda** And the same on Saturdays, I suppose?
**Monica** Saturdays are worse. We don't close till eleven.
**Rhoda** But that is sixteen hours. That means an eighty-four hour week.
**Monica** Yes. Before Christmas we had a whole week of sixteen hour days. We never got to bed till one in the morning.
**Rhoda** And no half-day, of course?
**Monica** Oh no.
**Rhoda** What about holidays?
**Monica** A week in the summer.
**Rhoda** What do they pay you?
**Monica** Fifteen pounds a year.

*Mary returns with the tea*

**Rhoda** How long are your meal breaks?
**Monica** Twenty minutes. The worst thing is having to stand for so long. Sometimes I lose all feeling in my feet. Several of the girls have developed varicose veins. Some are dismissed because they are too weak.
**Virginia** I don't know how you have the strength.
**Monica** What else is there for me to do? I'm not brainy like you and Alice.
**Alice** You will soon find a husband, Monica. You are so pretty.
**Monica** What man will I ever meet? Only the ones who work in the shop, and they—The other day one of them tried to court me. He asked if we might not be on terms of friendship. I asked him how it would be possible for him to support a wife. "Not for some time," he replied, "but everyone hopes." What would have been the use of that—a long engagement, perhaps for years—even if I'd been attracted to him, which I wasn't? So many girls are persuaded into that kind of relationship. But how can I ever meet any other man? We have no brothers to introduce us to their friends. The only other possibility is strangers.
**Virginia** Monica! I hope you would never respond to any stranger who tried to speak to you.
**Monica** If he was a gentleman?

**Virginia** How could you be sure he was a gentleman? He might easily be an impostor. Or even if he was a gentleman he might have improper motives.
**Alice** Yes, indeed.
**Monica** Don't worry, Virgie. I can take care of myself.
**Rhoda** (*vehemently*) The whole concept is monstrous—that a woman should regard her future only in terms of marriage. There are half a million more women in England than men, who can therefore never find husbands. The pessimists call them lost, futile lives. They are wrong. Such women are a great reserve. They can work usefully as married women cannot.
**Monica** Married women are not idle.
**Rhoda** Some of them rock cradles and cook. Many do not even do that.
**Alice** (*timidly*) But what would you have these "other" women do?
**Rhoda** Become hard-hearted.
**Virginia** Hard-hearted? Why?
**Rhoda** So that they shall cease to regard marriage as a necessity.
**Monica** And children?
**Rhoda** Children too.
**Monica** Do you agree, Miss Barfoot?
**Mary** Yes. That is why we founded this school. To enable women to become independent. Rhoda and I went through what you did.
**Alice** But what can you train them to do except teach? And that profession is overcrowded already, as Virgie and I have learned.
**Mary** This. (*She goes over to the typewriter and sets it on the table before them*)
**Alice** (*a little fearfully*) What is that?
**Mary** A typewriting machine.
**Virginia** I have heard of them. Is that what they look like?
**Mary** There's a good deal of employment for women who learn to use them. Work in offices, or copying at home. With practice one can do fifty words a minute. Rhoda is a wonderful teacher. I am still rather slow myself.
**Alice** Fifty words a minute!
**Mary** Some people can reach twice that speed.
**Virginia** Great heavens!
**Monica** Can you show us?
**Mary** Of course. (*She types a sentence*)
**Virginia** Incredible! I could never learn to do that.
**Alice** Nor I.
**Mary** (*to Monica*) Could you?
**Monica** How long would it take me to learn?
**Mary** Six months.
**Monica** I'm afraid it's impossible.
**Mary** Why?
**Monica** How could I live for six months without earning anything?
**Mary** (*to Alice and Virginia*) Could she live with you?
**Virginia** Oh, dear. I'm afraid our little room barely has space for two. We have to share a single bed already. Unless——
**Mary** Yes.
**Virginia** There is another little room in the house which our landlady might let us have quite cheaply.

Act I, Scene 2                                                         9

**Mary** How much?
**Virginia** I think perhaps three shillings a week. But then there is food. Alice and I have accustomed ourselves to be vegetarians. But even that would cost another three shillings a week, and Monica would need more than we do.
**Monica** Why?
**Alice** Well, dear, you would be working all day at the school and that would make you hungry.
**Mary** I could lend you ten shillings a week.
**Monica** No, I could never accept that.
**Alice** Our dear father said we must never, never borrow.
**Mary** You could easily pay me back once you start earning.
**Monica** I don't know.
**Rhoda** You must say yes.
**Monica** It is very kind of you. But I must think it over. I would certainly be glad to leave the store.
**Rhoda** (*forcefully*) You must say yes.
**Monica** I must make up my own mind.
**Mary** Of course. (*She looks at her watch*) Well, I am delighted to have met you all.

*The others rise*

**Virginia** It has been so kind of you to see us.
**Alice** Yes, indeed. Monica, what a lucky girl you are.
**Monica** Thank you, Miss Barfoot. Good-night, Rhoda.
**Rhoda** Good-night, Monica.
**All** Good-night.

*Alice, Virginia and Monica leave*

**Mary** I wonder if she will agree to join us.
**Rhoda** Of course. Why should she not?
**Mary** Didn't you sense an unwillingness?
**Rhoda** She is simply fearful of giving up her job. As most women are.
**Mary** I thought there was something more than that.
**Rhoda** What?
**Mary** I'm not sure.
**Rhoda** Pathetic those sisters of hers are.
**Mary** Poor creatures. They were not made to battle with life.
**Rhoda** How much did they say their capital was? Eight hundred pounds? With that they could start a school of their own. We must suggest it to them.
**Mary** Do you think they are capable of running a school?
**Rhoda** It is surprising what women can do if they have to.
**Mary** But they don't have to.
**Rhoda** Yes, that's the problem. Oh, I sometimes wish girls would fall down and die of hunger in the streets instead of creeping back to their garrets and dormitories.
**Mary** You mean then people would try to reform things?

**Rhoda** Who knows? They might only congratulate each other that a few superfluous women had been disposed of.

**Mary** What shall I do about Bella?

**Rhoda** You have to choose between giving up the school or making it a refuge for outcasts. Let other people act the Good Samaritan. Our task is to train and encourage girls not to be husband-hunters. Do you imagine Bella won't fall for another man within six months?

**Mary** I suppose you are right. Very well, I will tell her that I cannot take her back. But, Rhoda, do you really know a single girl who believes in her heart that it is better never to love, and never to marry?

**Rhoda** Mary, Mary.

**Mary** I wonder if we don't damage our cause by demanding that a woman should deaden her sexual instinct.

**Rhoda** There must be a widespread revolt against sexual instinct if women are to be raised from their present level in society. Women's emancipation must have its ascetics as Christianity has. The way things are now, women imagine themselves noble and glorious when they are most animal.

## Scene 3

*Battersea Park*

*As in Scene 1. A boat is moored nearby. Widdowson sits waiting*

*Monica enters*

*Widdowson rises and raises his hat*

**Widdowson** I am so glad you were able to come.

**Monica** We are lucky with the weather.

**Widdowson** Yes, indeed. As it is so warm, I wondered if I might not invite you for a row on the river. I have hired a boat.

**Monica** (*genuinely pleased*) Oh, I would like that.

**Widdowson** I hoped you would.

*He helps her into the boat and takes the oars. It is something he is clearly skilled at*

**Monica** How different London looks from here.

**Widdowson** In what way?

**Monica** So much smaller. Don't you think so?

**Widdowson** Yes, you are right. And so peaceful.

**Monica** What is that red building?

**Widdowson** (*glances over his shoulder*) Chelsea Old Church. It is very fine inside. I believe Sir Thomas More used to worship there.

**Monica** Really?

**Widdowson** So I have heard. He used to live nearby. (*Pause*) You know, I still do not know your name.

**Monica** Monica Madden.

Act I, Scene 3                                                                 11

**Widdowson** Were you born in London?
**Monica** No, Somerset.
**Widdowson** A beautiful county. Do your parents still live there?
**Monica** Both my parents are dead.
**Widdowson** I am sorry. Have you any brothers and sisters?
**Monica** Two sisters. They are both a good deal older than me. They live at Lavender Hill.
**Widdowson** Are they married?
**Monica** No.
**Widdowson** Have they work?
**Monica** No. (*Pause*) Oh, this is so beautiful, being out here. I feel miles and miles away from Wandsworth. It's like being in the country again. At the seaside. It's so long since I saw the country, or the sea.
**Widdowson** (*after a moment*) I was very much afraid that I would not see you today.
**Monica** I promised to come if it was fine.
**Widdowson** I feared you might change your mind.
**Monica** Why should I have?
**Widdowson** I thought you might be unwilling to spend a longer time with someone so much older than you. I must be over twice your age.
**Monica** I don't find anyone interesting to talk to at the shop. And I don't meet anyone else. That is——
**Widdowson** Yes?
**Monica** There is a lady named Rhoda Nunn whom we used to know when we were children. She and a friend of hers called Miss Barfoot have started a school to teach women how to typewrite, so that we can find office work or copying. They have offered to take me on as a pupil and lend me enough to keep myself for the six months that the course will take.
**Widdowson** That sounds an excellent plan. It will be far better than working in the shop, surely.
**Monica** Miss Nunn is a remarkable person. She is the first woman I have met who is daring enough to think and act for herself. She is quite like a man, so energetic and resourceful. I never imagined that one of our sex could plan and act as she does. Miss Barfoot founded the school—she has the money. But it is obviously Miss Nunn who runs it.
**Widdowson** When will you start there?
**Monica** I don't think I shall.
**Widdowson** Why not?
**Monica** Miss Nunn is such a powerful personality. So grand and demanding. I don't think I could live up to her ideals. To put myself into her hands might be a worse kind of bondage than what I suffer at the shop. Am I being stupid?
**Widdowson** On the contrary. You are very prudent and far-sighted for your years. Will you think me rude if I ask how old you are?
**Monica** Twenty.
**Widdowson** And I am forty-four.

SCENE 4

*Mary's house in Chelsea*

**Mary** Everard should be here soon.
**Rhoda** Who?
**Mary** My cousin.
**Rhoda** I thought you said he was in Japan.
**Mary** He has come back. Didn't I tell you?
**Rhoda** No. You seem to be keeping open house today.
**Mary** You know I try to discourage people from visiting me on weekday evenings. I feel so tired after a day at the school. I haven't your energy, Rhoda. Well, I'm ten years older than you are.
**Rhoda** Everard. Isn't he the black sheep of the family?
**Mary** Yes. No. I'm not sure. He was thought to be.
**Rhoda** You seem excited about meeting him again.
**Mary** He was different from the others.
**Rhoda** Tell me about him.
**Mary** Well, his father was a self-made man. He sent Everard to Eton.
**Rhoda** Oh dear.
**Mary** Which turned him into a Radical.
**Rhoda** You make him sound rather admirable.
**Mary** He was. If he'd found a congenial occupation, I think he would have achieved something. But he seems to have no ambition.
**Rhoda** Strange for a Radical.
**Mary** His Radicalism evaporated.
**Rhoda** Ah. Yes, it fits. I still don't see how this makes him a black sheep, except in his father's eyes.
**Mary** There was a scandal.

*Rhoda roars with laughter*

You find that funny?
**Rhoda** Which was it? An affair with a married woman, an illegitimate child, or an abortion?
**Mary** It was an illegitimate child. But it may not have been his, he says.
**Rhoda** (*laughs again*) The usual excuse. What men get away with! Has he ever married?

*The doorbell rings*

**Mary** No.

*Mary goes to the door and admits Everard Barfoot. He is thirty-five, handsome, relaxed and courteous*

**Everard** Cousin Mary.
**Mary** Cousin Everard.

Act I, Scene 4                                              13

*They embrace affectionately*

This is my partner Rhoda Nunn.
**Everard** How do you do.
**Rhoda** Good-evening.

*They sit*

**Everard** Well, Mary. It's been a long time.
**Mary** Ten years, I think.
**Everard** Yes, it must be. (*Pause*)
**Rhoda** (*rises*) You two will have private matters to discuss.
**Mary** (*a little nervously*) No, please stay, Rhoda.

*Rhoda sits*

**Everard** You said that Miss Nunn is your partner. In what, if I may ask?
**Mary** A school.
**Everard** Really? How old are the pupils?
**Mary** Eighteen to twenty, mostly.
**Everard** Advanced education. You and Miss Nunn must be very learned people.
**Mary** It depends what you mean by advanced—and learned. We teach them to typewrite.
**Everard** Ah. Yes, I have heard of that machine. It hasn't reached Japan yet. They are rather backward industrially. Cling to the past, as I'm sure you know. It sounds a useful invention. May I become a pupil?
**Mary** I'm afraid not.
**Everard** Oh? Why?
**Mary** Our school is for young women.
**Everard** I see. Are there such schools for men?
**Mary** Of course. Are you thinking of learning?
**Everard** I might.
**Rhoda** You don't strike me as a typical Old Etonian.
**Everard** I hope I am not. I hate those bloody aristocrats. And the snobbery. I refused to go to university.
**Rhoda** So what did you do?
**Everard** I enlisted at one of these new polytechnics, to study engineering. My father disinherited me.
**Rhoda** One might have expected him to approve. I gather he was self-made.
**Everard** Oh, he'd reacted against all that. He didn't want to be reminded that he'd risen from the ranks.
**Rhoda** So you are an engineer?
**Everard** Not any longer. I soon found I had no talent for it. Not the mathematics, for one thing. But I stuck it out till I was thirty because I didn't want to admit to my father that I'd been wrong.
**Mary** What are you planning to do now?
**Everard** I really have nothing in mind. I managed to save quite a bit in the East. Enough to be independent in a modest way. So now I intend simply to enjoy life.

**Mary** At your age?

**Everard** So young, or so old, do you mean?

**Mary** So young, of course. Surely you do not want to waste your life?

**Everard** Oh, I shan't waste it. For twelve years I have worked as hard as any man. I don't pretend I enjoyed it, because I was in the wrong profession. I could never have reached the top. I found no self expression in it.

**Rhoda** Should you not try to find some work through which you could express yourself?

**Everard** Of course you are right. But there is so much I want to see and do first. When I was in the East I took every opportunity to travel. I used my holidays to go everywhere I could—China, the East Indies, Siam, Burma, the South Seas. I saw more than most men see in a lifetime. But it made me realize how much there is left to see. Europe alone would fill more years than I shall live. And then there is Africa and the Americas, and countries I only glimpsed, like India. How many other men have the opportunity to travel as I can, now that I don't need to stay in one place and earn a living?

**Mary** You haven't thought of marrying?

**Everard** I'm not sure that I ever shall. Oh, not for the reason you're thinking. I should like to have a home and children. It's just that most marriages seem so unhappy. Put your hand on your heart, Mary, and tell me how many really happy marriages you know. (*Pause*) Or you, Miss Nunn.

**Rhoda** Very few, if any. But the main reason lies in the attitude of men. They expect their wives to be completely subservient, and to have no life of their own except being a wife and a mother. They don't understand that women need to express themselves as much as men.

**Everard** Exactly. And the worst thing is that women meekly accept this. I couldn't be happy with a woman who only wanted to be subservient to me. My wife would have to be as independent-spirited as I am. Of course such people exist. But for two equally independent-minded people to live together seems to me an almost certain recipe for disaster. To live alone would surely be a lesser evil.

**Rhoda** I agree. But a man can do that and satisfy his sexual needs. A woman cannot unless she is willing to lose her good name. Society accepts promiscuity in a man but not in a woman.

**Everard** So what is the answer?

**Rhoda** The only answer is for a woman to rise above her animal instincts.

**Everard** But then the human race would die out.

**Rhoda** No, because most women would prefer even an unhappy marriage to celibacy. At least marriage gives them a home of their own instead of a hired room. And most women have no vocation except to be a wife and mother. It should not be so, but it is. When I say a woman should rise above her sexual instincts, I am speaking only of the minority, who have some other vocation. If they marry they have to surrender that, unless their work is something they can do at home, like writing. But name me a great female writer who has also been a mother.

**Everard** But cannot an independent-spirited woman enter into a free association with a man and damn what society thinks of her, like George Eliot did with George Henry Lewes, or George Sand with Chopin?

Act I, Scene 4                                                                 15

**Rhoda**  That is all right if your name is George. Seriously, a reputation for immorality may even increase their selling power. But how many pupils do you think Mary and I would have left if it became known that either of us was living with a man to whom we were not married? How many patients would a woman doctor keep? How many businessmen would employ such a woman?
**Everard**  And yet there must be some solution. (*He looks at his watch*) Cousin Mary, I must be going.
**Mary**  So soon?
**Everard**  I have to see an old friend at seven. (*He laughs*) I made the appointment because I was uncertain how you would receive me. This has been delightful. I hope I may see you soon again.
**Mary**  Of course.
**Everard**  And you, Miss Nunn.
**Rhoda**  (*non-committally, but not coldly*) Good-night, Mr Barfoot.
**Mary**  I'll see you out.
**Everard**  Good-night Mary.
**Mary**  Good-night.

*Mary and Everard go*

*Rhoda lights a cigarette*

*Mary returns. She seems emotional and upset*

*Rhoda notices, but does not speak*

**Mary**  (*at length, lights a cigarette*) Well. What do you think of my wicked cousin?
**Rhoda**  Quite interesting.
**Mary**  He is certainly much improved.
**Rhoda**  I pity the woman who marries him, though.
**Mary**  Why?
**Rhoda**  I find it hard to believe him when he says he wants an independent-minded wife. He is too soft. In the end he will choose someone who will obey his wishes and flatter his vanity. And bear his children.
**Mary**  If he marries anyone.
**Rhoda**  Oh, I think he will. At heart he's a conformist, don't you think?
**Mary**  Perhaps you're right. I'm not sure. I've always had a feeling of guilt towards him.
**Rhoda**  Why on earth?
**Mary**  Because the money which Everard should have inherited, his father left to me. Without that I couldn't have started my school.

*Mary is silent for a moment. Rhoda does not interrupt her thought*

**Rhoda**  Come on, let's make supper.

*Rhoda exits, leaving Mary alone*

## Scene 5

*Battersea Park*

*Widdowson and Monica are in the boat*

**Widdowson** As you will have gathered, I lead a very quiet life. For years I lived in lodgings. All my life I longed to have a home of my own. When I got it last year I was like a child with a toy. I used to walk all over it day after day even before it was furnished. There was something that delighted me in the sound of my footsteps on the staircases and the bare floors.

**Monica** I can imagine.

**Widdowson** I kept saying to myself: "Here I shall live and die." But not, I hoped in solitude. Was it possible, I wondered, that I might meet someone . . . ? I do not expect you to give me an immediate answer to what I am about to ask. But I should like you to consider the possibility of becoming my wife.

**Monica** Mr Widdowson!

**Widdowson** The difference between our ages is great, but I know of several couples where the same difference exists and yet who are happily married. I sometimes wonder whether that is not a better basis for marriage than that the two should be of the same age. A man is calmer and more tolerant at forty than at twenty-five or even thirty, and—how shall I put it?—less likely to stray emotionally. I am sure I could be happy with you, and I ask you to consider whether you might not find happiness with me.

*Monica is silent*

Will you permit me to show you—and your sisters—my home?

**Monica** I don't know.

*Pause*

**Widdowson** At least let me hope that you will be here again next Sunday?

**Monica** I don't know.

**Widdowson** I shall be here at all events. (*Pause*) I know this must have come as something of a shock to you.

**Monica** I have never thought of you in such terms. Not for a moment.

**Widdowson** I am sure. But please consider—a good home—a man who shares your interests and will always love and respect you—and be a good father to your children.

**Monica** I must go. My sisters are expecting me.

**Widdowson** Will you allow me to drive you there? Or to drop you somewhere on the way?

**Monica** No. Thank you. No.

*She climbs ashore, Widdowson assisting her*

**Widdowson** Next Sunday?

*She walks away in silence*

Act I, Scene 6                                                                 17

SCENE 6

*Mary's house in Chelsea*

*Rhoda is alone, typing. The doorbell rings*

*Rhoda admits Monica*

**Rhoda** Good-evening.
**Monica** Good-evening. Please forgive me for coming without an appointment.
**Rhoda** Not at all. I am pleased to see you.

*Rhoda indicates a chair. They sit*

**Monica** Actually, it was Miss Barfoot I came to see.
**Rhoda** I am afraid she is out for the evening. Can I help?
**Monica** (*uncertainly*) Er—yes.
**Rhoda** You want to complete arrangements about joining the school?
**Monica** Well, no.
**Rhoda** Has some problem arisen?
**Monica** Someone has asked me to marry him.
**Rhoda** Ah. And you have accepted him?
**Monica** Not yet. But I think I shall.
**Rhoda** How long have you known him?
**Monica** I have only met him three times.
**Rhoda** And he swept you off your feet and you are madly in love with him.
**Monica** Not at all. He is over twice my age and I do not love him. But he is the only man I have met who treats me like a human being.

*Pause*

**Rhoda** If this were one of your sisters speaking, I could understand. They have nothing else to live for—unless they put their capital into starting a school, which they never will. Almost any marriage would relieve their present state of hopelessness. But you, Monica! You are not like them. This is exactly what you must not do. You are spirited and independent— you showed that by going to work behind a counter. You can achieve something in life. You must not surrender that for the sake of a comfortable home. You'll regret it bitterly some day.
**Monica** Oh, Rhoda, you're wrong about me. I *am* like Alice and Virgie at heart. I have their nature, I am weak and childish. I admire Miss Barfoot and you, but I can't go your way. I want to have children. More than anything else.
**Rhoda** But this man is much too old for you. Your habits and his won't suit.
**Monica** He promises me I shall live exactly the life I please. He says that will please him.
**Rhoda** But you do not love him.
**Monica** I respect and like him.

**Rhoda** That is not the same as loving someone.
**Monica** What man am I ever likely to meet whom I could love?
**Rhoda** Monica, once you have finished our course and started work you will come in touch with a different class of men—in an office, or people who will bring you copying work—writers, perhaps, all kinds of new people.
**Monica** I thought you distrusted love between man and woman.
**Rhoda** I do. Men fall out of love—as they call it—quickly. They start looking for another partner.
**Monica** Then perhaps it is better to marry someone one does not love. I think Mr Widdowson and I could have a good life together. A good marriage. Would that not be better than living with a man who in time would cease to love me, and take a mistress or hanker after other women?
**Rhoda** It is better not to marry at all.
**Monica** For you, perhaps. And Miss Barfoot. Not for me.

*Pause*

**Rhoda** Do you have some other reason for not wanting to join our school?
**Monica** What other reason could I have?

*Pause*

**Rhoda** So, your mind is made up?
**Monica** Yes.

*Rhoda stands up. Monica does the same*

Oh, Rhoda. Wish me happiness.
**Rhoda** I can't wish you that, because you are not looking for happiness. But I wish you contentment.

*The doorbell rings. Rhoda goes to open it*

*Everard stands there*

**Everard** Good-evening.
**Rhoda** (*surprised and unwelcoming*) Good-evening.
**Everard** I happened to be in the neighbourhood, so I thought I might drop in. But——
**Monica** I am just leaving.
**Rhoda** Not on my account, I hope.
**Monica** No, I was going anyway. Good-night, Rhoda. Good-night, Mr——?
**Everard** Barfoot. Good-night.

*Monica goes*

**Rhoda** Mary is out for the evening.
**Everard** Oh. I'm sorry.
**Rhoda** She will be here next Sunday, as far as I know. Shall I tell her you will be calling then?
**Everard** If you would. (*Pause*) Since I am here, may I request the pleasure of a few minutes conversation with you? I have been thinking a lot about some of the things you said and would greatly like to discuss them further. If you have the time.

## Act I, Scene 6

**Rhoda** (*glances towards the typewriter*) I am rather busy. But—Please sit down. Can I offer you a glass of sherry?
**Everard** Thank you.

*She pours a glass for him, hesitates, then pours one for herself*

May I ask who was that young lady?
**Rhoda** Her name is Monica Madden.
**Everard** One of your pupils?
**Rhoda** No. I used to know her when she was a child. I am rather annoyed with her.
**Everard** Oh? Why?
**Rhoda** She is a bright and intelligent girl who is about to throw her life away by marrying a man more than twice her age. She doesn't love him and hardly knows him, but despairs of meeting anyone more suitable.
**Everard** Why on earth? She seemed quite pretty.
**Rhoda** She works behind the counter in a shop and never meets any men of her class or intelligence. Like most middle-class girls who have no brothers and no inheritance. I wanted her to join our school. Mary even offered to lend her money to cover her training. But the temptation of a comfortable home seems to be too much for her.
**Everard** Couldn't she even wait six months?
**Rhoda** Apparently not.
**Everard** Extraordinary. Dear, oh dear. A man twice her age whom she doesn't know——
**Rhoda** I think there may be another reason why she doesn't want to join the school.
**Everard** What?
**Rhoda** I have a feeling that she is scared of me. That I might prove more dominating than this man she plans to marry.
**Everard** But it would only be for six months. Then she would be free of you.
**Rhoda** (*after a pause*) I think she is afraid she might become dependent on me.
**Everard** But what a prospect! Marriage is a bad enough business anyway, but a man she doesn't even pretend to love——
**Rhoda** She thinks the best recipe for a lasting marriage is with someone you don't love.
**Everard** Why?
**Rhoda** Because love fades.
**Everard** And mutual respect need not. I suppose there's logic in that. It would be a fair enough reason for marrying at forty, or even thirty-five. But to have reached that conclusion at—she can't be more than twenty——
**Rhoda** She says an older husband would be less likely to be unfaithful.
**Everard** But what if she meets the man of her dreams? Then her reasoning will go out of the window.
**Rhoda** She seems set on it. She is a determined young woman, though strangely enough she regards herself as weak.
**Everard** Yes, I have found that in several women. They will not admit that

they are strong, as though that were something shameful—unwomanly. God, it must be terrible to be a woman in our society.

**Rhoda** (*passionately*) Oh, no! We have one great advantage. A woman with brains and *will* can play a part in the most important movement of our time. The emancipation of our sex.

**Everard** You speak as though it was a new religion.

**Rhoda** It is. The most important religion. I thank heaven every day that I was born a woman.

**Everard** Yes, I know it's splendid to have a crusade. You are right. (*He laughs*) Men have always kept women subservient and done their best to deny them higher education, and then we complain that they make uninteresting life companions.

**Rhoda** Yet you will marry some time. Even though you know you will be less happy than as a bachelor.

**Everard** No. Marry in the legal sense I never shall.

*Rhoda laughs scornfully*

Oh, please don't misunderstand me. I would welcome a lasting relationship, with a woman of character and brains. But she would have to be as independent of social conventions as I am myself.

**Rhoda** You mean, live with you unmarried?

**Everard** Yes. I don't of course advocate this for everyone. A free union presupposes equality. One could only propose it to a woman who could understand all that was involved, and would be prepared to resume her separate life if that became desirable. The brutality of enforced marriage doesn't seem to me an alternative worth considering. Nor would it appeal to any woman of the kind of which I speak.

**Rhoda** And what if she has a child? You know that until a safe form of female contraceptive can be found, women will never be safe from pregnancy.

**Everard** Or a form of male contraceptive that is not so thick that it halves the pleasure.

*Rhoda grimaces*

Forgive me, I should not have said that.

**Rhoda** No, I have heard that before from women. They are aware of it too, you know. But I am not really interested in this aspect of the subject. My work is only for women who eschew relationships with men.

**Everard** And you are prepared to eschew the two things most men and women long for—love, and children?

**Rhoda** As Monica said, love fades. Nine times out of ten.

**Everard** You don't agree that it is better to have loved and lost——?

**Rhoda** No.

**Everard** And children?

**Rhoda** They are not always an unmixed blessing. You must know, as I do, households where the parents do not even like their children, nor their children them.

**Everard** I do.

Act I, Scene 6                                                                21

*The clock strikes*

Well, I must be going. I have enjoyed our conversation.
**Rhoda** So have I.
**Everard** May I look forward to another?
**Rhoda** If you wish. Mary and I are usually in on Sundays, as you know.
**Everard** Thank you. Good-night.
**Rhoda** Good-night.

*He takes her hand. She does not withdraw it. He kisses it, in such a way that she cannot take offence. As he does so:*

*Mary enters, distressed*

**Everard** Good-evening, Mary.

*Mary does not answer. She takes off her hat and coat and throws them on a chair*

**Rhoda** Mary, what's the matter?
**Mary** Everard, would you mind leaving us?
**Everard** Of course. Good-night.

*Everard goes*

**Mary** (*looks at Rhoda*) Bella Royston has hanged herself.
**Rhoda** I am sorry to hear that.
**Mary** You should be sorry.
**Rhoda** We took the correct decision.
**Mary** How can you possibly say that? The girl has died the most horrible death. And she was not evil, or in any way bad, just weak and perhaps foolish. Whom did she ever harm except herself?
**Rhoda** You agreed that if we took her back the school would close. You gave her money.
**Mary** It wasn't money she needed. She needed help. More than that. She needed what you so despise, love.
**Rhoda** Our school, if it survives, will give hope and a meaning in life to scores, perhaps hundreds, of women who otherwise would have had none. Is one death, however regrettable, not a price worth paying for that?
**Mary** No. Oh, Rhoda, you have hardened your heart with theory. If one is to work for women one must keep one's womanhood. You are becoming—you are wandering as far from the true way as—oh, much farther than Bella did. This hardness is not natural in you. You are warping your true nature.
**Rhoda** I am only trying to be honest. You speak of warping. Your emotions are warping your judgement. It is not only the women who attend and will attend our school. Many, perhaps most of them will have a similar influence on others to what we have done for them. It cannot be allowed to fail. Other instances like Bella's are bound to arise. We have to be single-minded. Ours is a crusade. If we weaken, we fail. Your conscience is misleading you.
**Mary** Can a conscience ever mislead?

**Rhoda** Of course. How would a commander ever win a battle if he bothered about some of his men being killed?
**Mary** Your logic may be correct.
**Rhoda** You know it is.
**Mary** But it is not a logic that I can live with. I don't know if we can continue to live together.
**Rhoda** You must decide that.
**Mary** (*suddenly embraces Rhoda*) Oh, Rhoda.

*Mary kisses her. Rhoda kisses her back coolly, then goes to the table and begins to type*

SCENE 7

*Alice's and Virginia's room*

*Monica enters*

*Virginia comes to greet her. Alice remains seated*

**Virginia** Dearest Monica! Many happy returns of the day.
**Monica** (*kisses her*) Thank you, Virgie. Hullo, Alice.
**Alice** You mustn't come near me.
**Monica** Why not?
**Alice** I have a bad cold.
**Monica** Oh, Alice, I'm sorry.
**Alice** You mustn't catch it.
**Monica** I'll take the risk. (*She kisses her*)
**Alice** (*pleased*) Oh! You're a naughty girl.
**Virginia** We have a small present for you. (*She hands her a parcel*)
**Monica** Oh, you shouldn't. What can it be? (*She unwraps a book*) "The Christian Year". How lovely.
**Alice** They are such beautiful poems. I never cease to find comfort in them.
**Virginia** Mr Matthew Arnold said there was nothing to equal them in English.
**Monica** Thank you. Oh, my dears, thank you. (*She kisses them*) Now I have some news for you.
**Alice** What can that be?
**Virginia** I know. You have started at the typewriting school.
**Monica** No.
**Alice** Tell us, tell us. We are on tenterhooks.
**Monica** I am going to get married.

*Uncertain silence*

**Virginia** Married? Oh, Monica.
**Alice** But how can you have met—? Is it someone at the shop?
**Monica** No. His name is Edmund Widdowson. He is very comfortably off and has a beautiful house of his own on Herne Hill.

**Virginia** (*claps her hands*) Herne Hill! That is a very fashionable locality.
**Alice** How did you meet him? Was he a customer?
**Monica** No. We met quite by chance, in Battersea Park.
**Virginia** (*worried*) Battersea Park?
**Monica** Yes. I was reading a book. He was resting his horse and asked me what I was reading.
**Alice** That was very forward of him, surely?
**Virginia** I am surprised you answered him.
**Monica** He was not at all forward, quite the contrary. He was very shy, and apologized for approaching me.
**Alice** How many times have you met him?
**Monica** Three.
**Virginia** Only three? And you feel—you feel you know him well enough to take such a step?
**Alice** Forgive me, dearest Monica, but are you sure you are not—not just infatuated with him? Young men can be so deceptive.
**Monica** He is not young. He is forty-four.
**Alice** Forty-four?
**Virginia** Is he a widower? I trust he is not divorced?
**Monica** No, he has never married.
**Virginia** Do you love him?
**Monica** No. But I think I could have a good life with him. He promises me I shall live as I please. And Alice, Virgie. He has promised to help you.
**Alice** Help us?
**Monica** He says he will give you as much each year as you have already.
**Virginia** Oh, Monica! (*She claps her hands*) As much again as we have now! We shall be able to eat fish, and—and meat.
**Alice** We can take a second room.
**Virginia** We shall live like royalty. Oh, Monica! How happy we shall all be!

SCENE 8

*Chelsea Gardens*

*Rhoda is seated, reading*

*Everard comes to her*

**Everard** (*raises his hat*) Good-afternoon, Miss Nunn.
**Rhoda** Good-afternoon.
**Everard** I have just called at the house, but was told that my cousin is not well.
**Rhoda** She has a headache.
**Everard** Oh! Do you know what caused it?
**Rhoda** She had to attend an inquest this morning. I think it upset her.
**Everard** That former pupil of yours?
**Rhoda** Yes.

**Everard** I read about that. It must have upset you too.
**Rhoda** No.
**Everard** No?
**Rhoda** It had no effect whatever on me.
**Everard** Forgive me if I say that I find that difficult to believe——
**Rhoda** Are you charging me with falsehood, Mr Barfoot?
**Everard** I only meant that perhaps you won't allow yourself to admit——
**Rhoda** I cannot admit what I don't feel. I will bid you good-afternoon.

*She holds out her hand. He retains it*

**Everard** You must, you shall forgive me. I shall be too miserable if you dismiss me in this way. I see that I was wrong. You know all the particulars of the case and I have only seen a brief newspaper report. I am sure the girl didn't deserve your pity. You do pardon me?
**Rhoda** Please don't be foolish. I will thank you to let my hand go. We are in a public place.
**Everard** (*releases it*) Will you have the kindness to tell me whether that was the only cause of my cousin's unwellness?
**Rhoda** I can't say. I haven't spoken with her for two or three days.
**Everard** You haven't seen each other?
**Rhoda** Miss Barfoot is angry with me. I think we may be obliged to part.
**Everard** Why?
**Rhoda** If I must satisfy your curiosity, Mr. Barfoot, she blames the girl's death on me, for persuading her that it would be wrong to take the girl back. We have had a painful conversation. I don't know that we can continue to live together.
**Everard** I am sure you and she will get over it. Won't you let me try to persuade her that she is wrong?
**Rhoda** How do you know that she is wrong?
**Everard** I respect Mary's judgement, but I respect yours more.

*She does not respond*

I was so pleased to find you here. It is over a week since that second time we met, and I couldn't keep away any longer.

*She remains indifferent*

(*After a pause*) You know, of course, that I am in love with you.
**Rhoda** I am very sorry to hear it. Happily, the sentiment will not long trouble you.
**Everard** I am more serious than you give me credit for. The sentiment, as you call it, has troubled me ever since I met you, and will last. I want you for the companion of my life. I don't see very well how I can do without you. You can picture the kind of life I want you to share. My wife, or my lover, would be as free to live in her own way as I in mine. But make no mistake, it is love that I am asking for, because I believe that the mutual love of a man and a woman who can think intelligently and respect each other may be the best thing that life has to offer.

Act I, Scene 8                                                                                         25

*Rhoda has been smiling in a forced way with her lips close-set*

**Rhoda**  As you insisted on speaking, I had no course but to listen. It is usual, I believe, if one may trust the novels, for a woman to return thanks when an offer of this kind has been made to her. So—thank you very much, Mr Barfoot.

*Everard takes a chair, seats himself on it beside Rhoda and takes one of her hands rapidly and vehemently*

**Everard**  I will have no such thanks. You shall understand what it means when a man says that he loves you. I have come to think your face so beautiful that I am in torment with the desire to press my lips upon yours. When I first saw you, I thought you interesting because of your evident intelligence. Nothing more. I did not think of you as a woman. Now you are the one woman in the world.

*Pause. She does not try to withdraw her hand*

Can you love me in return? Am I anything like this to you? Have the courage you boast of. Speak to me as one human being to another.

**Rhoda**  I don't love you in the least. And if I did I would never share your life.

**Everard**  Why not? Because you have no faith in me?

**Rhoda**  I can't say whether I have or not. But I have my work, and no-one shall ever persuade me to abandon it.

**Everard**  But suppose marriage in no way interfered with your work?

**Rhoda**  It would interfere. What would become of the encouragement I am able to offer our girls?

**Everard**  Encouragement to reject marriage?

**Rhoda**  To reject the old idea that a woman's life is wasted if she does not marry. My work is to help those women who are forced by circumstances to live alone. Vulgar opinion ridicules them—calls them old maids. How can I help them better than by being one of them? If I deserted them, I should despise myself.

**Everard**  Magnificent! If I could bear the thought of living without you, I would bid you persevere and be great.

**Rhoda**  Then for your own peace I must hope that you will avoid me. It is so easily done. We have nothing in common, Mr Barfoot.

**Everard**  I can't agree with that. There are not half a dozen women living with whom I could talk as I have talked with you, and it isn't likely that I shall ever meet another. Am I to abandon the one chance of perfecting my life?

**Rhoda**  You don't know me. We differ profoundly on a thousand essential points.

**Everard**  I do not look for repose. I seek the mutual incitement of vigorous minds. Life should be a battlefield, not a bed of roses.

*Pause*

**Rhoda**  I gather that you are a father.

**Everard**  Ah. Mary told you that?

**Rhoda**  She and I have no secrets from each other. Do you think it was wrong of her to tell me?

**Everard** No. But she does not know the full story, because I have not told her. Do you wish to hear it?
**Rhoda** Not particularly.
**Everard** I shall tell you nevertheless, and you may believe it or not as you please. It happened ten years ago. The girl's name was Amy Drake. She made a pass at me, I succumbed, she became pregnant and demanded that I marry her. I was not her first man by any means, and I could not be sure that the child was mine. So I refused. The child died. Should I have married her? (*Pause*) Do you believe me?
**Rhoda** How can I without having heard the other side?
**Everard** Which you will never hear.
**Rhoda** Precisely. And I don't know you well enough to take your word on trust.
**Everard** I love you, and I can't abandon hope.
**Rhoda** I shall not continue with this conversation. We have spoken in this way for the last time. Good-afternoon, Mr Barfoot.

*Rhoda goes*

**Everard** Odd creature!


## Scene 9

*Widdowson's house*

*Widdowson and Monica are making preparations for a soirée. Widdowson stands awkwardly by while Monica finalizes arrangements with Alfred, the manservant*

**Monica** Is everything ready now, Alfred?
**Alfred** I think so, madam.
**Monica** It all looks beautiful. Mrs Gibson and you have done very well.
**Alfred** Thank you, madam.
**Monica** Don't you think so, Edmund?
**Widdowson** Yes, very nice.

*Alfred leaves*

**Widdowson** Well, this is our first at-home. I feel quite nervous.
**Monica** So do I.
**Widdowson** I am afraid your friends will find me rather dull.
**Monica** Nonsense. They will like you.
**Widdowson** I know so little about women's emancipation. And I suppose that is what they will mainly talk about.
**Monica** Not at all. They have wide interests. They are both great readers.
**Widdowson** But mainly I imagine in sociology and politics. I know nothing about either subject. And you know how shy I am with strangers.
**Monica** They will like you for that. Everyone likes shy people.
**Widdowson** Well, I don't know.

Act I, Scene 9                                                                 27

**Monica** Oh, by the way, Mary has sent a note asking if she may bring her cousin Everard. Of course I said yes.
**Widdowson** What does he do?
**Monica** He used to be an engineer.
**Widdowson** (*encouraged*) Ah. What does he do now?
**Monica** Apparently he has retired.
**Widdowson** He is older than her, then.
**Monica** No, younger actually.
**Widdowson** Has he come into money?
**Monica** I don't know. He worked in the East for ten years. In Japan, mainly.
**Widdowson** Ah, that sounds interesting. (*He looks at her*) I am so proud of you, Monica.
**Monica** Thank you, Edmund.
**Widdowson** To be able to entertain in my own house, with a beautiful young wife. I do not know what I have done to deserve it. (*He kisses her*) I love you very deeply.
**Monica** (*evades his embrace*) Do we offer them food at once, or should we let them drink for a while first?
**Widdowson** You know how inexperienced I am in these matters. Is it important?
**Monica** Probably not.
**Widdowson** We must do what is correct. Oh dear. We should have thought of this.
**Monica** Alfred will know.
**Widdowson** My dear, we cannot ask a servant what is correct.
**Monica** Nonsense. (*Calls*) Alfred.
**Widdowson** Monica! You should have rung for him.
**Monica** I'm sorry, Edmund.

*Alfred enters*

Alfred, should we offer the guests food at once or let them drink first?
**Alfred** It is not customary for guests to start eating as soon as they arrive, madam.
**Monica** Thank you, Alfred. Offer them food when you think fit.
**Alfred** Strictly speaking, madam, and with respect, you should ask them. If you wait half an hour or so——
**Monica** Half an hour? Very well.

*The doorbell rings*

**Alfred** Excuse me, madam.

*Alfred goes and returns with Alice and Virginia*

Miss Madden and Miss Virginia Madden.
**Monica** Alice! Virgie! (*She kisses them*)
**Alice** I do hope we are not late. We had a long wait for the omnibus at Charing Cross.
**Monica** Of course not, you're the first.
**Widdowson** Good-evening.

**Alice** Good-evening, Edmund.
**Virginia** Good-evening.
**Alfred** Red or white wine, madam?
**Alice** Oh. White, thank you.
**Virginia** Red, please.

*They take a glass and their eyes turn towards the buffet*

**Alice** What a magnificent spread. Did Mrs Gibson do all that?
**Monica** Yes.
**Virginia** It must have taken her hours.
**Monica** Yes. Do sit down, now.

*Disappointed, they sit*

**Alice** Oh, Monica, what a lucky girl you are. Such a beautiful home.
**Monica** Yes, I am very lucky. Everyone tells me so.
**Virginia** And to have a husband with such exquisite taste.
**Monica** Yes.
**Widdowson** Now, you are flattering me.
**Virginia** Indeed I am not. I was saying to Alice only yesterday, Edmund has exquisite taste. I do not know a more tastefully decorated house.
**Widdowson** Well, I had nothing else to think about really at the time. So I put my whole mind to it.

*The doorbell rings*

*Alfred goes to answer it*

**Alice** Who else is coming?
**Monica** Just Miss Barfoot and Rhoda. And a cousin of Miss Barfoot, a Mr Everard Barfoot. He is lately returned from ten years in Japan.
**Virginia** Japan! How very exciting.

*Alfred enters*

**Alfred** Miss Mary Barfoot. Miss Rhoda Nunn.

*Mary and Rhoda enter*

**Monica** Good-evening, Miss Barfoot.
**Mary** Good-evening. But you must stop calling me Miss Barfoot.
**Monica** (*smiles*) Mary. Good-evening, Rhoda.
**Rhoda** Good-evening, Monica.
**Monica** This is my husband, Edmund.
**Widdowson** }
**Mary** } (*together*) Good-evening.

*Widdowson and Rhoda exchange "Good-evenings". Alfred offers them drinks. A ring at the door*

**Alfred** (*to Monica*) Excuse me, madam.

*Alfred goes and returns with Everard*

Act I, Scene 9  29

Mr Everard Barfoot.

*Monica and Widdowson greet him and introduce him to Alice and Virginia*

**Rhoda** (*to Mary, vexed*) You didn't tell me he was coming.
**Mary** Didn't I? I am sorry. I thought you liked him.
**Rhoda** He is intelligent, but can be tiresome.
**Mary** In what way?
**Rhoda** He fancies himself irresistible to women.
**Mary** But he does it quite agreeably, don't you think?
**Rhoda** He certainly has charm. And knows it.
**Mary** (*amused*) Rhoda! Has he been courting you?
**Everard** (*comes over*) Good-evening, Mary. Miss Nunn.
**Mary** Good-evening.
**Rhoda** Good-evening.
**Widdowson** (*joins them*) Miss Barfoot, my wife has been telling me about your school. It sounds a most worthy enterprise.
**Mary** I think it serves a purpose. Of course we meet a good deal of resistance.
**Widdowson** How so?
**Mary** Many men say that by entering the commercial world we unsex ourselves.
**Widdowson** Ah.
**Mary** And damage the chances of men finding work. And reduce salaries, because a woman can be paid less than a man.
**Widdowson** I see.
**Rhoda** They say we injure our own sex by making it impossible for men to marry who, if they earned enough, would be supporting a wife.
**Widdowson** They have a point there.
**Rhoda** They ask why we don't confine ourselves to the half-dozen occupations which are deemed strictly suitable for women. Why don't we encourage them to become governesses or hospital nurses.
**Widdowson** Surely those are both admirable careers?
**Rhoda** Indeed.
**Widdowson** And are they not more—forgive the phrase, but are they not more womanly than office work?
**Rhoda** By womanly, you mean work that a man disdains. You are asking us to keep to our proper world.
**Widdowson** Oh, I——
**Rhoda** No. A new type of woman must emerge, active in every sphere of life. A new worker out in the world, a new ruler in the home.
**Widdowson** (*disturbed*) Ruler in the home?
**Rhoda** Oh, by all means let us keep the old virtues associated with women. But let us add to them the virtues hitherto thought appropriate only to men. Let a woman be gentle, but at the same time let her be strong. Our natural growth has been stunted. Let us free ourselves from the heritage of weakness and contempt.
**Monica** (*comes over*) What are you four talking about?
**Widdowson** Miss Barfoot and Miss Nunn have been explaining their philosophy. It has been most instructive.

**Monica** Come and talk to Alice and Virginia, or they will feel neglected.
**Widdowson** You know how difficult I always find it to make conversation with them.
**Monica** Mary, you come and help him.
**Mary** Of course.

*They go to Alice and Virginia, leaving Rhoda and Everard together*

**Everard** I'm so glad you and Mary are still together.
**Rhoda** Women can discuss things sensibly too, you know.
**Everard** I am afraid you frightened our host.
**Rhoda** Is that a bad thing?
**Everard** By no means. What a stiff fellow he is. I pity Monica having to live with him.
**Rhoda** It was her choice. Why in God's name couldn't she have waited? If she had to marry at all.
**Everard** Would you rather she'd stayed in the dormitory above the shop, on an eighty hour week for fifteen pounds a year? And she had no prospects, none.
**Rhoda** At least she was free there.
**Everard** Free to do what? Widdowson obviously dotes on her—look, he can't keep his eyes off her. And I dare say she wears the trousers.
**Rhoda** Disgusting phrase.
**Everard** I'm sorry. But don't you think she gets her way most of the time?
**Rhoda** But she will achieve nothing in life.
**Everard** No, you are right there. You are beginning to convert me.
**Rhoda** Well, well.
**Everard** How long do you think it will take for women to achieve equality in this country?
**Rhoda** True equality, probably never.
**Everard** Why do you say that?
**Rhoda** Because most women will always opt for marriage and children. Which will prevent them from giving their full time to other work. So there will always be far more men in any field outside the home. But we shall make gains. The vote, for instance. I think I shall live to see us get that. And women in Parliament. Maybe women barristers.
**Everard** What about women judges?
**Rhoda** (*laughs*) That will be the day!
**Everard** At least they are now allowed to attend universities.
**Rhoda** As poor relations. We are less enlightened than the Greeks. Even Plato admitted women to his Academy. Unlike that fathead Aristotle.
**Everard** What did Aristotle think?
**Rhoda** He said our principal virtue was obedience.
**Everard** So Mr Widdowson is an Aristotelian.
**Rhoda** (*laughs*) Undoubtedly.
**Everard** Tell me, have you ever been abroad?
**Rhoda** No.
**Everard** That surprises me.

## Act I, Scene 9

**Rhoda**  I never had the money. And since Mary and I started the school, I have not had the time.
**Everard**  The East would fascinate you.
**Rhoda**  I am sure.
**Everard**  I was disappointed at first. I'd read so much of the magic of the East, and all I could see was ugliness and squalor.
**Rhoda**  So, what would fascinate me? Where does the magic lie?
**Everard**  It's a different attitude towards time. You become conscious of the hugeness of things. I mean, compared with man—and woman. What seems important here doesn't seem so there.
**Rhoda**  Meditation and all that. I don't think that would appeal to me. I want to be doing.
**Everard**  It doesn't mean you have to be inactive. You can combine the two. It's not like our so-called religion, when people go to church as a social ritual. Easteners often don't worship in public at all. They have a little shrine in their house, just a fireplace or a shelf, no more. And there they put anything that they have come across in the day that seems to them beautiful or to have meaning. A piece of wood they found on the pavement, an oddly shaped stone. You become aware of a kind of candle flame behind their eyes. And you hope to light one behind yours.
**Rhoda**  And did you?
**Everard**  Yes. Only a small one as yet, tiny. But I hope it will grow.
**Rhoda**  Mr Barfoot, you are flirting with me again.
**Everard**  Of course.
**Rhoda**  You are a strange man. Fundamentally selfish, aren't you? A materialist, a sensualist. And yet you speak of candle flames.
**Everard**  I don't think one should deny one's sensuality. I think that diminishes one. Of course it should not become dominant. But one is a less complete person without it.
**Rhoda**  It can be a distraction. From what is important.
**Everard**  Not if one has it under control.

*The women go to the buffet and are served by Alfred*

(*To Widdowson*) This is a beautiful house, Mr Widdowson. You have furnished it charmingly.
**Widdowson**  Thank you.
**Alfred**  Supper is ready, madam.
**Monica**  Thank you, Alfred. Everybody please come and eat.
**Everard**  You are in the City, I understand?
**Widdowson**  Yes. That is, I am semi-retired. I have a partner who manages the business very ably.
**Everard**  What kind of business, if I may ask?
**Widdowson**  We are timber importers.
**Everard**  Softwood or hardwood?
**Widdowson**  Softwood. You know the field, then?
**Everard**  I learned something about it during my stay in the Far East.

*The Lights fade and then fade up. Everard is talking to Monica, watched by Widdowson and Rhoda. Monica is listening to him animatedly*

I assure you it isn't much fun to be a wife in those countries. Compared with them, England is almost emancipated. A man in Malacca once said to me: "If I come home and find that my wife and my mother have quarrelled, I do not wonder which is right. I know that my mother is right".

**Monica** (*laughs*) Oh, my goodness!

**Everard** Yes, I wouldn't recommend any European woman to marry into the community there. If ever you feel depressed, count your blessings. I don't of course mean——

**Monica** No, I am very lucky in my husband.

**Mary** Rhoda, I think we should be going.

**Rhoda** What time is it? (*She looks at her watch*) Good heavens. I had no idea it was so late.

**Mary** (*glances towards Everard*) Has the time flown?

**Rhoda** (*non-committally*) Yes. Good-night, Mr Barfoot.

**Everard** Good-night, Miss Nunn. Good-night, Mary.

**Mary** Good-night. (*To Monica and Widdowson*) Thank you. It has been a lovely evening.

**Monica** It has been exciting for us. Our first at-home. I was so nervous.

**Rhoda** You managed everything beautifully. Good-night, Mr Widdowson. Thank you.

**Widdowson** Good-night, Miss Nunn. Miss Barfoot.

**Mary** Everard, will you share our cab? We are going in the same direction.

**Everard** Thank you. Good-night, Mrs Widdowson. Mr Widdowson. (*He bows to Alice and Virginia*)

*Everard, Mary and Rhoda go*

*Alice and Virginia show no signs of leaving*

**Monica** Another glass of wine, Alice? Virgie?

**Alice** } (*together*) No, thank you, Monica.
**Virginia** } Thank you. It is a very nice wine.

*Alfred refills her glass*

**Monica** Some more salmon? Or pie?

**Alice** } (*together*) Thank you.
**Virginia** }

*Alfred gives them some. They eat avidly. For some seconds nothing is said*

**Alice** What an exciting evening.

**Virginia** Yes, indeed.

**Alice** Such lovely food. And you say Mrs Gibson did it all herself?

**Monica** Yes.

**Alice** She is a treasure. It is not easy to find such excellent cooks nowadays, I am told.

**Monica** No.

**Virginia** And such exquisite wine.

**Widdowson** I like to keep a good cellar.

**Virginia** (*slightly tipsy*) Oh, Monica, how fortunately things have turned out for you. To be able to entertain on this scale.

Act I, Scene 9 33

**Monica** Yes.
**Virginia** Have you—have you any other news for us?
**Monica** What kind of news?
**Virginia** Any—news? Er . . . ?
**Monica** I don't think so. Have we, Edmund?
**Widdowson** I don't think so. Oh, I have bought a new horse for the trap.
**Virginia** (*disappointed*) Oh, that is interesting.
**Widdowson** A good chestnut.
**Alice** Ah. (*Pause*) Well, Virgie, I think we should be going. If we are not to miss our train.
**Virginia** (*glances towards the buffet*) Oh, do we have to?
**Alice** I think we should. (*Gets up*) Thank you, Monica dear. (*She kisses her*) It has been an evening to remember. Thank you, Edmund.
**Monica** You must both come again soon.
**Widdowson** Indeed. Yes. Good-night, Virginia.
**Virginia** Aren't you going to finish your glass, Alice?
**Alice** No, I've really drunk enough.
**Virginia** It's a pity to waste it. May I? (*She drains Alice's glass*) It really is delicious.
**Monica** Alfred, see my sisters to the station, please. Then you can go to bed.
**Alfred** Very good, madam.
**Alice** There's really no need. It's only a few minutes walk.
**Monica** No, it's a dark road. (*She kisses them both*) Good-night, Alice. Good-night, Virgie.
**All** Good-night.

*Alice and Virginia exit with Alfred*

**Monica** Poor, stupid Virgie.
**Widdowson** You are charitable. This is not the first time we have seen her like this.
**Monica** She is very unhappy. Alice and she have so little to live for.
**Widdowson** That is hardly an excuse for getting drunk in someone else's house.
**Monica** I'm sorry.
**Widdowson** Well, it is not your fault. But I think in future we should only invite them to tea.
**Monica** What did you think of the others?
**Widdowson** Mr Barfoot is cultivated and courteous. He had much of interest to tell me about the Orient. And was surprisingly well-informed about the timber trade. I noticed that you had a long tête-à-tête with him.
**Monica** Yes, I found him interesting too. What did you think of Mary and Rhoda?
**Widdowson** They are clearly able-minded and energetic persons.
**Monica** Poor Edmund. Did they alarm you?
**Widdowson** They didn't alarm me. I found them unfeminine.
**Monica** Not your idea of what a woman should be?
**Widdowson** Exactly.
**Monica** You'd rather a woman should be subservient, and know her place?

**Widdowson** Since you ask me, yes. I do not find it natural that an educated woman should seek to imitate the life of a man.
**Monica** We don't want to imitate the life of a man. We just want to be allowed to be individuals.
**Widdowson** Do I not allow you that?
**Monica** No. Oh, Edmund, you're kind and generous to me——
**Widdowson** I thought I had given you everything you want.
**Monica** Materially, yes. But I would like more freedom. To go out by myself when you are at the office—visit galleries, go to concerts.
**Widdowson** You may do that, Monica, with a chaperon.
**Monica** Chaperon! Edmund, I'm not a child.
**Widdowson** No respectable woman walks around London without a chaperon. What else do I deny you?
**Monica** I want to read books that haven't been approved by you. I'd like to join a Women's Society.
**Widdowson** Women's Society!
**Monica** Where we can discuss things.
**Widdowson** What kind of things?
**Monica** Social questions, and politics.
**Widdowson** Politics! What has a woman to do with politics?
**Monica** They interest me.
**Widdowson** They should not.
**Monica** I want something to think about. What is wrong with that?
**Widdowson** Monica, a woman has her sphere and some things lie outside it. It is Miss Barfoot and Miss Nunn who have put these ideas into your head.
**Monica** They only crystallized what was already there.
**Widdowson** Well, I think they are a bad influence on you. I would prefer that you do not associate with them. It is they who have given you this unnatural desire for independence. You used to have no such thoughts. They have poisoned your mind. I have given you a home, a good home, and you should be content with that.
**Monica** Are you forbidding me to see them again?
**Widdowson** I would prefer that you didn't.
**Monica** You are unreasonable. Certainly I shall continue to see them.
**Widdowson** Then I must forbid you. If you do see them it will be in defiance of my wish.
**Monica** Than I shall have to defy your wish.
**Widdowson** Monica, Monica, don't you love me?

*She does not reply*

(*Falls on his knees, clasps her waist, sobs*) Monica, my darling, my beautiful wife. Have you no love for me? Have you begun to hate me?
**Monica** Please get up, Edmund.
**Widdowson** I was so violent, so brutal with you. I spoke without thinking.
**Monica** But why do you speak like that? Why are you so unreasonable? If you forbid me to do simple, harmless things, you can't expect me to take it like a child. I shall resist—I can't help it.
**Widdowson** (*clasps her*) I want to keep you all to myself. I don't like these

Act I, Scene 9

people. They think so differently—they put such hateful ideas into your head. They are not the right kind of friends for you.

**Monica** You misunderstand them, and you don't in the least understand me. Oh, you hurt me, Edmund!

**Widdowson** (*releases her, takes her hand in his hands*) Monica, I would rather you were dead than that you should cease to love me. You may go to see these women. But, Monica, be faithful, be faithful to me.

**Monica** Faithful to you? What have I done to make you fear that I should not be? I simply want to make new friends——

**Widdowson** It's because I have lived so much alone. I have never had more than one or two friends, so I feel jealous when you want to get away from me and amuse yourself with others. I can't talk to such people. I am not suited for society. If I hadn't met you in that strange way I should never have been able to marry. If I allow you to have these friends——

**Monica** *Allow*? Do you think of me as your servant, Edmund?

**Widdowson** It is I who am your servant, your slave.

**Monica** How can you say that? It is you who forbid and allow and command——

**Widdowson** I will never again use such words. Only convince me that you love me as much as ever, Monica. Say you love me.

*She is silent*

You can't say that you love me?

**Monica** I am always showing it. Don't be so foolish, Edmund. You must either trust me completely or not at all. If you can't and won't trust me, how can I possibly love you?

**Widdowson** Yes. I see. Well, my dearest, choose something that you would like to do.

*Monica thinks*

**Monica** I would like to visit the exhibition at the Royal Academy. You know it would bore you, Edmund. So let me go there by myself one afternoon while you are at the office.

*Widdowson hesitates*

**Widdowson** Very well.

**Monica** Thank you.

**Widdowson** (*clasps her and kisses her*) Oh, Monica. You have given me such happiness. If only we could—if only we could——

**Monica** (*disengages herself*) Edmund, please.

**Widdowson** Forgive me. I only meant—I pray every night that God will bless our marriage with a—with a——

*He does not see the look of revulsion which crosses her face*

# ACT II

## Scene 1

*The Royal Academy*

*Monica is looking at the paintings. So, separately, is Everard*

**Everard** (*raises his hat*) Mrs Widdowson.
**Monica** Mr Barfoot.
**Everard** What a pleasant surprise. Thank you for that delightful evening last week.
**Monica** I hope everything went all right. It was our first at-home. Edmund and I were both very nervous.
**Everard** Everything was faultless. Delicious food, excellent wines, and a model hostess.
**Monica** You are flattering me.
**Everard** No, I mean it. I was pleased to meet your sisters too. I liked them both.
**Monica** (*slightly embarrassed*) Thank you.
**Everard** I am surprised that neither of them has married. They are good-looking women. Or could be if they believed in themselves.
**Monica** They never met any man who appealed to them. How could they as a governess or a lady's companion?
**Everard** Miss Nunn thinks they should open a school. I gather they have some little capital. That would not only give them something to do, but would broaden their acquaintance. They would meet all kinds of people, and might even find suitable husbands.
**Monica** I am afraid they have given up hope.
**Everard** Of finding husbands?
**Monica** Of anything.

*Widdowson appears on the far side of the stage and watches them without being able to overhear them*

Have you ever been married, Mr Barfoot?
**Everard** No.
**Monica** Why is that?
**Everard** I have never met a woman I wanted to marry. Until a few weeks ago.
**Monica** And now you will?
**Everard** I don't think she will have me.
**Monica** Why not?
**Everard** She disapproves of marriage.
**Monica** Oh, dear. Is she an emancipationist?
**Everard** Yes.
**Monica** (*not meaning anything*) Like Miss Nunn?
**Everard** Yes.

Act II, Scene 1                                                               37

**Monica** (*after a moment*) Good heavens.
**Everard** You find that surprising? That I should be in love with her?
**Monica** A little.
**Everard** She is more of a mystery to me than any woman I have known. I don't know if she will ever reveal herself to me. If she does I feel it would be the strangest revelation. Every woman wears a mask, but Rhoda's—Miss Nunn's—is a completer disguise than any I have tried to pierce. Do you think she is capable of falling in love?
**Monica** She would perhaps try not to admit it to herself.

*Widdowson's features have become twisted with jealousy*

**Everard** When in fact it had happened?
**Monica** She would think it nobler to disregard such feelings.
**Everard** Yes. She wants to be an inspiring example to the women who cannot hope to marry. She would be ashamed to take a contrary course.

*They move along the rows of paintings*

*Widdowson slips out*

**Monica** Yes. She despises me for having married. She regards it as a sign of weakness, especially if one is not in . . . (*She stops, embarrassed*)

*Everard does not complete her sentence, though he knows it*

I think Miss Nunn is very strong. She frightens me a little.

*Harry Bevis, twenty-nine, good-looking and bohemianly dressed, enters. He is roughly the same build and colouring as Everard*

**Everard** Was that why you chose not to become one of her pupils?
**Monica** Yes. I don't really know her, though, not really. A woman can be as much of a mystery to another woman as she is to a man.
**Bevis** (*to Everard*) It's worse this year than ever.
**Everard** Really?
**Bevis** (*with contempt*) Have you seen the latest Alma-Tadema?
**Everard** No.
**Bevis** Aren't you going to introduce me?
**Everard** I'm sorry. This is my new neighbour, Mr Bevis. He lives in the flat above mine. Mrs Widdowson.
**Bevis** How do you do.
**Monica** How do you do.
**Everard** (*looks at his watch*) I must be going, if you will excuse me. Goodbye, Mrs Widdowson. I have enjoyed our conversation.
**Monica** So have I.
**Everard** Goodbye, Bevis.
**Bevis** Goodbye.

*Everard leaves*

You are interested in painting, Mrs Widdowson?
**Monica** Yes. And you?
**Bevis** Yes. I paint myself.
**Monica** Indeed?

*Bevis points silently to a painting*

Is that by you?
**Bevis** Yes.
**Monica** (*after a moment*) It is very powerful. And unusual.
**Bevis** I am afraid that means you don't like it.
**Monica** (*looks at it again*) It is so different from what I am used to. So—blurred.
**Bevis** I have been studying for some years in Paris. They have a new method there. They aim to show how something looks, not when you survey it calmly, but at the moment when it first strikes you. I saw this landscape from a train, rushing past me, and this is how I remember it.
**Monica** You mean you painted it from memory?
**Bevis** Yes. A moment's remembered impression. And the train itself I painted as it might have been seen by someone standing in a field—the speed, the blur of the wheels, the vibration, the passengers glimpsed through the windows. Like a photograph when the subject has moved. Or trees photographed in a high wind.
**Monica** (*looks at it*) Yes, I see. Yes. Now you have explained it to me, I understand. Have you any other paintings here?
**Bevis** No. I was surprised they accepted this, it is so unlike what the Royal Academy usually shows.
**Monica** What a pity. I should like to see more of your work.
**Bevis** Would you really?
**Monica** Yes.
**Bevis** My sisters are coming to tea with me tomorrow afternoon. Why don't you come too, if you are free? I think you would enjoy meeting them. I live not too far from here. (*He hands her his card*) You know Chelsea?
**Monica** (*looks at it*) A little. Yes, I think I know this street.
**Bevis** Four o'clock?
**Monica** (*hesitates*) I am not sure if I should.
**Bevis** If your husband allows you to visit the Academy unchaperoned, he would surely not object to your joining my sisters and me for tea?
**Monica** (*smiles*) Very well.
**Bevis** Four o'clock, then?

## Scene 2

*Widdowson's house*

*Widdowson alone, restless. The front door opens and closes*

*Monica enters, happy*

**Monica** Good-evening, Edmund.
**Widdowson** Good-evening. You are late.
**Monica** I didn't leave here till late.
**Widdowson** Why was that?

## Act II, Scene 2

**Monica** I was finishing a book. I'm in good time for dinner.
**Widdowson** A husband likes his wife to be waiting for him when he returns from work.
**Monica** Well, I'm sorry.
**Widdowson** How was the Academy?
**Monica** Very interesting.
**Widdowson** Nobody bothered you?
**Monica** Of course not.
**Widdowson** Did you see anyone you knew?

*Monica hesitates*

**Monica** Yes, Mr Barfoot.
**Widdowson** Did he speak to you?
**Monica** Of course.
**Widdowson** Why of course?
**Monica** It would have been discourteous of him if he hadn't, since he was our guest last week.
**Widdowson** It is a strange coincidence that you and he should happen to visit the Academy at the same time.
**Monica** Do you think so?
**Widdowson** How long did you speak with him?
**Monica** I really don't know. About ten minutes, I dare say. What on earth is wrong with that?
**Widdowson** A man does not like his wife being seen speaking alone with another man in a public place.

*Monica makes a gesture of annoyance*

Oh, Monica, you are ignorant of the world.
**Monica** As you think a woman should be.
**Widdowson** Some kinds of knowledge are harmful to a woman. A married woman must accept her husband's opinion, at all events about men. A man may know with impunity what is dangerous if it enters a woman's mind.
**Monica** I don't believe that. I can't and won't believe it. You are being totally unreasonable. Last night you said you did not wish me to go on seeing Mary and Rhoda. Now you do not want me to speak with Mr. Barfoot. You said you found him interesting. So do I. I am going upstairs to change for dinner.
**Widdowson** We shall finish this conversation first, if you please.
**Monica** (*sits*) Very well.
**Widdowson** You have said several times how much you miss Somerset. The countryside, and the sea. I suggest that we sell this house and move there.
**Monica** What about your work?
**Widdowson** My partner can easily take care of everything. It will be enough if I go in once or twice a month.
**Monica** What about Alice and Virgie? I am the only friend they have in London.
**Widdowson** I will buy them a cottage in the neighbourhood. They will be company for you.

**Monica** The only company I shall have.
**Widdowson** You do not regard me, your husband, as company?
**Monica** Not when you behave like this. You are merely my jailor.
**Widdowson** Monica!
**Monica** Edmund, be honest. You want me to go with you to a quiet country place where I shall be under your eyes every moment. Why don't you say so plainly? What other motive have you?
**Widdowson** We differ hopelessly. We used to be able to discuss these things in a friendly spirit. Now you say whatever you know will irritate me.
**Monica** I want to be your friend. But you won't let me.
**Widdowson** My friend! No more than that? You have lost all love for me?

*She does not reply*

Yes, you no longer love me.
**Monica** Do you ever ask yourself whether you try to make me love you? You are always either angry or complaining.
**Widdowson** What did Barfoot say to you this afternoon?
**Monica** (*takes a deep breath*) I shall not tell you.
**Widdowson** You refuse!
**Monica** I could tell you. Every word. But I will not. I will only say that you might have heard every syllable and not taken offence. No, let me finish. You are being weak and unmanly. Things will never be better between us until you start thinking of me as your free companion, not your bondwoman. If you can't do this it will not be possible for us to go on living together.
**Widdowson** (*after a pause*) Very well. I shall allow you this freedom, as you call it.
**Monica** Thank you.
**Widdowson** But not in London. Tomorrow I shall take the train to Somerset to look for a house. Oh, Monica, it is only this accursed London that has come between us. The air has never suited you. All our trouble has stemmed from your ill health. Now, this is a fair bargain, is it not? We shall move to Somerset, and once we are there, you shall have your freedom. (*He kisses her*) You will see, my darling. Our second year of marriage will be very different from our first.


SCENE 3

*Mary's house*

*Rhoda is typing. Mary watches her from a chair. Rhoda seems distracted. Her typing slows, then stops. Mary opens her purse and tosses a coin on to Rhoda's table*

**Rhoda** (*picks it up*) What is this?
**Mary** A penny.
**Rhoda** I can see that. Why?

## Act II, Scene 3

**Mary** For your thoughts.
**Rhoda** Actually, I was thinking about the Lake District.
**Mary** You'll enjoy yourself there. You're not having doubts?
**Rhoda** It's so long since I took a holiday. I'm not sure I shall enjoy it.
**Mary** You'll love it, and it will do you good. You'll walk and read. It'll refresh you no end.
**Rhoda** (*unconvinced*) Yes.
**Mary** Is there something else?
**Rhoda** Nothing important.
**Mary** It's Everard, isn't it?
**Rhoda** That damned cousin of yours. Yes.
**Mary** Has he got under your skin?
**Rhoda** He's tiresome. But yes, he does interest me. Against my better judgement.
**Mary** Yes?
**Rhoda** He could become something worthwhile. Or he could just fritter away his life. I don't know why it should bother me.
**Mary** It always does, when one comes across someone in that situation.
**Rhoda** Mm.
**Mary** How do you find it, to have a man in love with you?
**Rhoda** (*dismissively*) Love, love.
**Mary** He has told you, of course?
**Rhoda** Oh, he says so. But you know men. It can mean anything.
**Mary** In his case, I think it means a lot.
**Rhoda** Has he spoken to you about it?
**Mary** No, but I can tell.
**Rhoda** Men have loved you, I suppose?
**Mary** Oh, yes. But none for whom I felt anything.
**Rhoda** And you only loved once?
**Mary** Yes.
**Rhoda** Who was he?
**Mary** Never mind. How do you feel about Everard?
**Rhoda** I don't trust him.
**Mary** And that is why you resist him?
**Rhoda** Oh, it's not the only reason. Mary, you know me. I distrust love, sex, whatever you want to call it. It's a distraction from what matters. And always leads to unhappiness in the end.
**Mary** And yet one has the feeling that one is not complete without it. Or anyway, without having experienced it, at least once.
**Rhoda** I could never be any man's wife. Whatever he promised. Look at poor Monica, and he seemed to promise everything. But to be a man's mistress, that would be impossible too.
**Mary** In a free association? Why?
**Rhoda** One might become emotionally dependent. That would be intolerable. And one's work would suffer, it would have to.
**Mary** Why?
**Rhoda** Because one's energy would be divided. And one's vision.
**Mary** It could broaden your vision.

**Rhoda** That's what I don't want.
**Mary** But you want to be loved?
**Rhoda** What makes you think that?
**Mary** Every human being does.
**Rhoda** But it would have to be for ever. If he ceased to love me—or I him—it would be the worst thing of all.
**Mary** That is the risk one has to take.
**Rhoda** I don't think I am prepared to. (*Pause*) He has asked to come and join me in Cumberland. Does that surprise you?
**Mary** No. What did you tell him?
**Rhoda** I said: "Provided that you accept that nothing can happen between us".
**Mary** And he agreed?
**Rhoda** Yes. But he would, wouldn't he? I shall have to write and put him off.
**Mary** You won't do that, will you?
**Rhoda** I don't know. Don't be silly, of course I shall. (*She looks at Mary*) I must. Otherwise I endanger all that we are working for.
**Mary** Well, it's up to you.
**Rhoda** There's no question of it.

*She starts to type again. Mary smiles*


SCENE 4

*Bevis's flat*

*Bevis is preparing tea. The doorbell rings. Bevis answers it*

*Monica is there*

**Bevis** Hallo. You found your way all right?
**Monica** Yes. It was quite easy.
**Bevis** I have a confession to make. My sisters cannot come.
**Monica** Oh.
**Bevis** I only received the news half an hour ago, so I had no opportunity to tell you. I do apologize.
**Monica** I see.
**Bevis** If you feel you cannot stay under those circumstances, I shall of course understand. Though I very much hope you will.
**Monica** I don't know. I should not.
**Bevis** You are afraid your husband would disapprove?
**Monica** It is not a question of whether he would disapprove. I make my own decisions.
**Bevis** As a woman should. (*Pause*) Let me take your coat. So, this is where I live.
**Monica** Very nice.
**Bevis** I have baked these scones for you. Do at least taste one.
**Monica** You made these yourself?

Act II, Scene 4    43

**Bevis** I like cooking. I learned in France.
*Monica, still without sitting, tastes one*
**Monica** This is delicious.
**Bevis** Thank you. Please don't eat the rest of it standing up.
*Monica smiles and sits. He pours the tea*
**Monica** Are all these paintings by you?
**Bevis** Not all of them. That and that. And that. Do have another.
**Monica** (*taking another*) Thank you. So, this is what an artist's home looks like.
**Bevis** Very untidy, I am afraid. I am sure your home is much more . . .
**Monica** Much more what?
**Bevis** Much neater and more gracious. I am sure you have furnished it exquisitely.
**Monica** My husband furnished it.
**Bevis** Oh?
**Monica** It was his before we married. So everything was there when I moved in.
**Bevis** He was married before?
**Monica** No, he lived on his own.
**Bevis** What does he do, if I may ask?
**Monica** He works in the City. That is—well, he is semi-retired now.
**Bevis** Already? That is rather young, surely.
**Monica** He is much older than me.
**Bevis** I see. Well, that often happens nowadays. You have children?
**Monica** No.
**Bevis** How about a piece of cake?
**Monica** Did you make this too?
**Bevis** Yes.
*Monica takes some and tastes it*
**Monica** You are really a very good cook.
**Bevis** Thank you.
**Monica** Are you married, Mr Bevis?
**Bevis** No.
**Monica** Why not?
**Bevis** I have never met anyone I wanted to marry. And I am happy on my own. I do not think one should marry unless one is in love. I know some people think that is old-fashioned. But it seems to me that to marry without at any rate supposing oneself in love is to abandon hope.
*Monica tries to reply but cannot. She bursts into tears*
 (*Putting his arm around her*) Don't cry. Please don't cry.
**Monica** I'm sorry.
*He kisses her on the forehead. She raises her face to his. They kiss passionately*
**Bevis** I don't even know your name.

**Monica** Monica. What's yours?
**Bevis** Harry.

*They kiss again*

**Monica** I must go.
**Bevis** Why?
**Monica** I must.
**Bevis** Please stay.
**Monica** No, I can't.
**Bevis** When shall I see you again?
**Monica** When would you like to see me?
**Bevis** Tomorrow? The same time.
**Monica** So soon?
**Bevis** Not soon enough.
**Monica** I can finish the cake, if it will keep.
**Bevis** I'll make you a new one.

## Scene 5

*Widdowson's house*

*Widdowson is alone*

*Monica enters*

**Monica** Hallo, Edmund. I'm sorry I'm late.
**Widdowson** Where have you been this afternoon?
**Monica** I went to see Alice and Virgie. Alice is unwell.
**Widdowson** What is wrong with her?
**Monica** Several things, I'm afraid.
**Widdowson** What?
**Monica** She seems to have no energy. They don't eat enough. She has these continual headaches.
**Widdowson** Has she seen a doctor?
**Monica** They say they can't afford it, but I've told them she must. I said we would pay for it.
**Widdowson** We?
**Monica** You. You don't mind, surely?
**Widdowson** I am glad you are so solicitous about your sister's health.
**Monica** I should be ashamed if I wasn't.
**Widdowson** (*shouts*) Liar!
**Monica** What do you mean?
**Widdowson** You were not at your sisters'. You were with that scoundrel Barfoot.
**Monica** Don't be ridiculous, Edmund.
**Widdowson** Do you deny it?
**Monica** Of course I do.

Act II, Scene 6                                                                 45

**Widdowson** Would you swear it on the Bible?
**Monica** If you wish.

*Widdowson takes a Bible, is about to offer it to her but puts it down*

**Widdowson** No. I shall not ask you to add perjury and blasphemy to the sin you have already committed.
**Monica** What sin?
**Widdowson** Adultery. Do not deny it further. I have had you followed.
**Monica** Followed?
**Widdowson** I had no alternative. I hired a person. He followed you to an address in Chelsea. My man saw Barfoot's name on the board in the hall. You stayed there over an hour. You were then seen coming down the stairs with a man exactly answering his description. Now will you confess the filthy truth?
**Monica** I tell you I have not seen or sought to see Mr Barfoot since we met at the Academy yesterday.
**Widdowson** You are the lowest of the low.
**Monica** I am telling you the truth.
**Widdowson** And what were you doing at that address if you were not with him? You go to the private chambers of an unmarried man. How long have you been dishonouring me? And yourself?
**Monica** I am not guilty of what you think. But I shall not try to defend myself. Thank God, this is the end of everything between us. Charge me with what you like. I am going away from you, and I hope we may never meet again.
**Widdowson** Yes, you are going—no doubt of that. But not before you have answered my questions.
**Monica** I shall answer no questions. All I want is to leave your house and never see you again.
**Widdowson** (*more softly*) You say you were never at that man's rooms before today?
**Monica** I shall answer no questions. Stay where you are! If you touch me I shall call for help until the servants come up. I won't endure your touch.
**Widdowson** Do you pretend that you are innocent of any crime against me?
**Monica** I am not what you called me. Explain everything as you like. I shall explain nothing. I want only to be free of you. I am going.
**Widdowson** You shall not leave this house.

*She walks past him through the door*


                                    SCENE 6

*The Lake District*

*Rhoda enters in walking clothes, her hair loose. She seems exhilarated by the exercise and the mountain air. She looks around her as though surveying the landscape*

*Everard, similarly dressed, appears on the other side of the stage*

**Rhoda** What are you doing here?
**Everard** I think you know.
**Rhoda** I told you not to come. You are very persistent.
**Everard** Rhoda, have pity on me.
**Rhoda** Pity—you? I would be the first woman who ever did.
**Everard** Because you are the first woman who has made me feel inferior.
**Rhoda** And that makes you think you are in love with me?
**Everard** Wouldn't you say it was as good a definition of love as any other?
**Rhoda** But then I cannot be in love with you, for I don't feel inferior to you.
**Everard** Oh, I don't say it's the only definition. One could love someone because they enrich your life. Or promise to enrich it. Deepen it, if you prefer. As I believe I could deepen yours.
**Rhoda** You might diminish it.
**Everard** I wouldn't, and you know I wouldn't. And if you found that I did, we could part.
**Rhoda** As you would if you got bored with me?
**Everard** If I ask fidelity from you, and I would, I should consider myself under the same obligation, whether we are legally married or not.
**Rhoda** Are you proposing legal marriage?
**Everard** Whichever you wish.

*Rhoda is silent. He takes a wedding ring from his finger and puts it on her finger. She removes it at once*

**Rhoda** Take it back, take it back, or I shall drop it in the heather. You want that old, idle form——
**Everard** Not the religious form. That has no meaning for either of us. Let us have a civil ceremony.
**Rhoda** If we can't trust each other without legal bonds, what is the point? I have said for years that women should not make marriage their goal in life. How can I continue to preach that with a wedding ring on my finger?

*Everard is silent*

Ah, I see. There would be many houses in which we would not be received.
**Everard** Exactly. And which would be the better for your school? You refused to take back Bella Royston because your pupils would leave and others would not join. Would not the same apply if you lived with me in a free union? Sacrifice your other principle for the sake of the more important good. You can still preach that marriage should not be women's main end in life even if you are married yourself. The argument would be more powerful coming from a married woman.

*Rhoda is silent for a moment*

**Rhoda** (*amused*) Damn you.

*He draws her to him and kisses her. She responds passionately*

**Everard** How extraordinary this landscape is.
**Rhoda** Yes.

Act II, Scene 7 47

**Everard** Such severity and gentleness. Those green hills—what could be more peaceful? But over there—those gorges and precipices. And that lake. So stern and black.
**Rhoda** Wastwater, yes. No one knows how deep it is. And those rocky heights that seem to frown on it.
**Everard** And this scent of peat. We shall never forget these things.
**Rhoda** No.

*They kiss again, long and deep*

## Scene 7

*Bevis's flat*

*The doorbell rings. Bevis admits Monica. They kiss*

**Bevis** I was afraid you wouldn't come.
**Monica** How could you think that?
**Bevis** I feared you might have second thoughts.
**Monica** Oh, no.

*They kiss again*

**Bevis** I've made you a ginger cake today. I hope you like ginger.
**Monica** I love it.
**Bevis** You're looking very beautiful.
**Monica** I feel beautiful when I'm with you. Yesterday was the first time for God knows how long. When I am with him I feel ugly.
**Bevis** How could you ever think that?
**Monica** He makes me feel soiled. His touch, and the way he looks at me.
**Bevis** My poor darling. Let's not talk about him.
**Monica** We must for a moment.
**Bevis** Why?
**Monica** Harry, do you love me?
**Bevis** Can you doubt it?
**Monica** I want you to think before you say it again. It's very important to me, you see.
**Bevis** I don't need to think. I love you, Monica.
**Monica** You must have known many women.
**Bevis** One or two.
**Monica** And being an artist—and living in Paris——
**Bevis** Yes, I have sowed my wild oats. I can't deny it.
**Monica** You won't want to commit yourself to one woman.

*Pause*

**Bevis** I could.
**Monica** Don't worry. I'm not asking you to do that. But——
**Bevis** Yes?
**Monica** Harry, I have left him.

**Bevis** Left your husband? On my account, you mean?
**Monica** No. Oh, yes, partly. I wouldn't have if I hadn't met you. Things came to a head last night. He told me he had hired a detective to follow me, and the man trailed me here.
**Bevis** But how could he have suspected——?
**Monica** He thought I was meeting Mr Barfoot.
**Bevis** (*uncertainly*) Why should he think that?
**Monica** I told him I had met Mr Barfoot at the Academy, the day I met you, and he—he's so insanely jealous. He said the vilest things to me. Called me a liar and an adultress.
**Bevis** He must be mad.
**Monica** When he said that, I suddenly knew what I had to do. It's strange, but I hadn't thought of it before. I had resigned myself to staying with him for the rest of my life. I sometimes thanked God that he was so much older than me that I might be free of him in twenty years. I prayed that he would not live to be old. Somehow it hadn't occurred to me that I might leave him. Well, last night I did.
**Bevis** He didn't try to stop you?
**Monica** Oh, yes. I told him that if he tried to prevent me physically I would shout so the servants would hear. That frightened him. I think he was more afraid of being humiliated before them than of my leaving him. I expect he thinks I'll come back after a few days, or that he can force me back. But I shan't go back to him, never.
**Bevis** Where did you spend last night?
**Monica** With Alice and Virgie. They were horrified, of course, and tried to persuade me I was wrong. They think I was lucky to find a rich husband and have all the things they'd like to have. And he makes them an allowance, so it'll be terribly hard for them—they'll have to go back to living in one room on seven shillings a week.
**Bevis** But how will you live? It won't be easy for you to find a job——
**Monica** Will you let me live with you?
**Bevis** Monica. He would sue you for divorce and name me as co-respondent.
**Monica** Would that bother you?
**Bevis** It would be very expensive for me and I'm not well off. Oh my darling, I don't want to sound materialistic, but——
**Monica** You said you have a place in Paris—
**Bevis** Just a room, in a friend's house.
**Monica** Is it big enough for two?
**Bevis** Well——
**Monica** Harry, I'm not asking you to marry me. I'm not asking for anything permanent. I just want to be with you for—oh, I don't mind if it's only for a few months. I want to find something I've never known—I don't know what to call it—joy. If you tire of me, I can move on. I can cope for myself, like I did before. (*Pause*) Do you despise me for coming to you like this?
**Bevis** Of course not. How could you think that?

*They kiss*

Oh, my dearest. (*He looks at her*) Dare you come with me to France?

Act II, Scene 7

**Monica** Dare I? What courage is needed? How dare I remain with a man I hate? Every day I have had to act the hypocrite. He has made me hate myself as much as I hate him.
**Bevis** Was he brutal to you?
**Monica** Only in the sense that he persuaded me to marry him—made me think I could love him when I didn't know what love meant. And then wanting to get me away from the few people I know because he is jealous. Jealous of everyone, even Rhoda and Mary because they give me something that he can't. But hasn't he cause for jealousy? I have deceived him, ever since we married, pretending to be a faithful wife when I only wished he might die and release me. I am to blame. I ought to have left him before. Every woman who thinks of her husband as I do ought to leave him. It is base and wicked to stay, pretending, deceiving——

*He takes her in his arms*

You love me, Harry? You will take me away with you?
**Bevis** Yes. Only one thing.
**Monica** Yes?
**Bevis** We mustn't travel together. They might trace us there.
**Monica** Oh, please let me go with you.
**Bevis** My own darling, think what it would mean if he found us. He'd drag us through every court—Can you stay with your sisters for a few more days? I shall need to make some arrangements. Do you love me? Do you really love me?
**Monica** How can you doubt it?
**Bevis** If you really love me——
**Monica** Harry, don't make me doubt *your* love. If I have not perfect trust in you, what will become of me? Oh, I am mistaken in you! You don't know what love means, as I feel it. You won't speak, you won't think, of our future together.
**Bevis** Monica, I have promised——
**Monica** Because I have come here, you think I have no sense of honour, no self-respect. Be honest with me. Would you rather I didn't come?
**Bevis** No, no. I couldn't live without you——
**Monica** Then why haven't you the courage to let everyone know it? Do you think we are acting wrongly?
**Bevis** No. I believe, as you do, that love is the only true marriage. Very well. Let us defy all consequences. For your sake——
**Monica** (*undeceived*) What is it you most fear? The scandal? The contempt that your mother and sisters would feel for you, perhaps not being able to see them again?
**Bevis** I shall have to endure that.
**Monica** I think I must go.
**Bevis** But what are our arrangements? Do you still intend——?
**Monica** Intend? Isn't it for you to decide?
**Bevis** Darling, do what I suggested at first. Stay a few days with your sisters till I am settled in Paris. A week at most, my darling.
**Monica** Very well, if you so wish it.

**Bevis** Say that you love me. I shan't rest until I can write and say "Come to me". Kiss me, Monica.

*She kisses him momentarily*

Like you kissed me before. What have I done that you should love me less? Tell me your love is unchanged.
**Monica** When we meet again. Not now.
**Bevis** You frighten me, Monica. We are not saying goodbye for ever?
**Monica** If you send for me I will come.
**Bevis** You promise?
**Monica** If you send for me, I will come.

*Monica goes*

Scene 8

*Mary's house in Chelsea*

*Mary and Widdowson*

**Widdowson** It is good of you to receive me, Miss Barfoot. I know how very busy you are.
**Mary** Please sit down.

*They sit*

What can I do for you?
**Widdowson** I hardly know where to begin. Something deeply upsetting has occurred. My wife has left me.
**Mary** Indeed?
**Widdowson** Two days ago.
**Mary** Well?
**Widdowson** I have reason to believe that she is conducting an—an *amour* with another man.
**Mary** But why do you come to me with this news? In what way can I help?
**Widdowson** The man in question is your cousin.

*Pause*

**Mary** Everard?
**Widdowson** Yes.
**Mary** Are you sure of this?
**Widdowson** I am afraid there can be no doubt. She denies it, but she would. I was compelled to hire a person to follow her. I had to, I had my reasons for suspecting her. My man followed her to the apartment block where he lives. She stayed for an hour, and a man answering his description was seen escorting her downstairs.
**Mary** But that need not mean that they——
**Widdowson** It was not the first time they were seen together.
**Mary** I am sorry to hear this.

**Widdowson** I was sure you would be.
**Mary** Sorrier than you know.
**Widdowson** I know how greatly he respects you. I wondered if you could perhaps have a word with him?
**Mary** You want her back? I promise you I will make him regret this.
**Widdowson** Thank you. I was sure you would.
**Mary** Thank you, Mr Widdowson.

SCENE 9

*The Lake District*

*Rhoda is alone*

*Everard enters*

**Everard** Well, Rhoda.
**Rhoda** Well.
**Everard** You summoned me.
**Rhoda** Yes.
**Everard** What an evening! It is as beautiful as when we met here before.
**Rhoda** Yes. We are lucky with the weather.

*He makes to kiss her but she puts her hands against his chest, and turns her head aside*

**Everard** I was restless to see you again.
**Rhoda** Were you, Everard?
**Everard** I haven't been able to get you out of my mind. You are there every hour, every moment.

*He turns her face to his. This time she does not resist, but after a second pushes him away*

**Everard** Why are you shy of me?
**Rhoda** There is a question I have to ask you.
**Everard** Ask it.
**Rhoda** Will you answer me truthfully?
**Everard** Of course. (*Pause*) What is it?
**Rhoda** Is there any woman—any woman living—who has a claim on you? A moral claim?
**Everard** No.
**Rhoda** None?
**Everard** None.
**Rhoda** Let me put the question another way. During the past month—the past three months—have you made profession of love—have you even pretended love—to any woman?
**Everard** Apart from you?
**Rhoda** Apart from me.
**Everard** No. (*Pause*) Have you any reason to disbelieve me?

**Rhoda**  Yesterday I received a letter from Mary. That was why I sent you the telegram, asking you to visit me.
**Everard**  From Mary? What did she say?

*Rhoda hands him a letter. Everard reads it*

(*Furious*) And you believe this?
**Rhoda**  Don't speak to me in that tone, please.
**Everard**  I am not one of your damned pupils. You insult me by showing me this letter.
**Rhoda**  (*equally furious*) What did you expect me to do. Tear it up?
**Everard**  Yes. That is what I would have done had I received such a letter about you.
**Rhoda**  It would hardly have been the same thing.
**Everard**  You mean, because I have known passion before and you have not?
**Rhoda**  (*flushes*) Passion! What right have you to make that accusation? Oh, I have known passion.
**Everard**  I thought you said you——
**Rhoda**  Not in your sense. Not for the flesh. Not like what you felt for Amy Drake.
**Everard**  Passion for things of the mind, you mean?
**Rhoda**  Of the soul. Do you think that inferior to your kind of passion?
**Everard**  You know I feel more than that for you.
**Rhoda**  Oh, you are clever. I have read and heard often enough of men like you. Why should she go to your rooms unaccompanied, not once but twice, on successive days? Why? Answer me.
**Everard**  No. I will not be cross-examined like this. If you will not believe me in this, how will you believe me in the future? You will suspect me of infidelity every time you see me talking to a woman, and nothing will convince you to the contrary. Jealousy, groundless jealousy——
**Rhoda**  (*laughs*) Groundless?
**Everard**  Why don't you ask Mrs Widdowson?
**Rhoda**  Could I believe her word, more than yours?
**Everard**  (*after a moment*) Have you changed your mind about me, and are you using this as an excuse?
**Rhoda**  (*passionately*) No.
**Everard**  Then we had better shake hands and part.
**Rhoda**  (*cold again*) If it seems so to you.

*They shake hands*

*Everard turns and leaves*

*She raises her hands to her face*

SCENE 10

*Mary's house in Chelsea*

*Mary is typing. After some moments, the doorbell rings*

Act II, Scene 10

*Mary admits Alice and Virginia*

**Mary** Good-evening.
**Alice** } (*together*) Good-evening.
**Virginia**
**Alice** It is very good of you to receive us.
**Mary** I could hardly refuse. You said you had something of the greatest urgency you wished to discuss with me.
**Virginia** Yes.
**Mary** What is it?
**Alice** We could not think of anyone else to ask, except you and Miss Nunn.
**Mary** You want to ask Miss Nunn also?
**Virginia** Yes. Not of course that we feel you could not advise us. It is only that——
**Alice** Miss Nunn has known Monica since she was a child, you see.
**Mary** (*coldly*) It concerns Monica?
**Virginia** Yes.
**Mary** I'm not sure that either Miss Nunn or I can help in any matter concerning her.
**Alice** Oh dear.
**Virginia** Of course she behaved very rashly——
**Mary** She did indeed.
**Alice** But now her situation is changed.
**Mary** Oh? How?
**Virginia** Is Miss Nunn—?
**Mary** Yes. (*Goes to inner door and calls*) Rhoda.
**Rhoda** (*off*) Yes?
**Mary** Could you spare a minute?
**Rhoda** I'm busy. Is it important?
**Mary** It may be.

*Rhoda enters. She looks as we first saw her, her hair forbiddingly up, without make-up*

**Mary** Alice and Virginia have something they wish to ask you.
**Rhoda** To ask me?
**Mary** About Monica.
**Rhoda** (*freezes*) I don't think I can be of any help concerning her.
**Virginia** Her situation is very difficult.
**Rhoda** Did she imagine it would not be?
**Alice** The man for whom she left Mr Widdowson has betrayed her.
**Rhoda** (*smiles*) Did he? Well, it does happen.
**Virginia** They had agreed to go away together. To France.
**Rhoda** France? How romantic.
**Alice** That is what she thought. But then she received a letter from him saying he did not think they should.
**Virginia** He said if he went through with their plan he would be acting selfishly and ruin her life.
**Rhoda** So what does she intend to do? Ask her husband to take her back?

**Alice** She may have to.

**Rhoda** That sounds the worst possible solution for both of them. Do you want me to urge her to do that, or not to do it? It is hardly something on which I——

**Virginia** You see, she is pregnant.

*Pause*

**Rhoda** By—this man?
**Alice** Oh, no.
**Rhoda** By whom, then?
**Virginia** Her husband, of course.
**Alice** There can be no-one else.
**Virginia** She has assured us that her love for the other man was pure.
**Rhoda** And you believe her?
**Alice** Why should she lie?
**Rhoda** To ensure that someone will pay for the child's upbringing.
**Virginia** No, that is unjust. Monica cannot lie.
**Rhoda** She seems to have lied to Mr Widdowson.
**Alice** That is true. But we are sure she is not lying in this. She loathes the very thought of seeing Mr Widdowson again. She says she would rather bring up the child on her own—that he should not know of its existence. But he is bound to find out and then he will not believe that the child is his, and what will become of it, and her? She cannot afford to have it unless he accepts responsibility.
**Rhoda** She is determined to have it?
**Alice** Of course.
**Virginia** Surely you are not suggesting . . . ? But that would be criminal. She might die, or go to prison.
**Rhoda** Would it be more criminal than bringing the child into the world? What kind of life can it expect?
**Alice** It has the right to live. It would be a sin to deprive it of that right.
**Virginia** It would be murder.
**Mary** You say she wishes to have the child, even if, as you say, it is her husband's, whom she loathes?
**Alice** Yes.
**Mary** Then I think her only choice is to ask Mr Widdowson to take her back. It will not be pleasant for either of them. But I see no real alternative.
**Rhoda** You assume he will accept that the child is his?
**Virginia** He must.
**Rhoda** You believe her because she has not lied to you. But she has lied to him. In his place, would you believe her? Every time he looked at the child he would wonder if it was his. His life and hers would be a misery, and what kind of a background would that be for the child to grow up in? With a father and mother whose mutual hatred was apparent every minute of every day?
**Alice** Will you at least see her? She very much wishes to speak with you.
**Virginia** She asked us to beg you to see her. Won't you please grant her that?
**Mary** I think you should, Rhoda.

## Act II, Scene 10

**Rhoda** I don't wish to see her. (*Pause*) Oh, very well.
**Virginia** Oh, thank you, thank you.
**Alice** God will bless you for this. Could I ask her to come in?

*Alice and Virginia go*
*Mary and Rhoda look at each other. Mary is about to speak*

**Rhoda** Don't say anything to me. (*Vehemently*) No, please.

*Mary goes*
*A knock at the door*

Come in.

*Monica enters*

**Rhoda** You have asked to see me.
**Monica** Yes. Thank you——
**Rhoda** I don't know that I can be of any help to you.
**Monica** Rhoda—Miss Nunn—will you tell me why you are behaving so coldly to me?
**Rhoda** Surely that doesn't need an explanation, Mrs Widdowson?
**Monica** You mean you believe everything that my husband has said?
**Rhoda** Mr Widdowson has said nothing to me. But I have seen your sisters, and there seemed no reason to doubt what they told me. Your affairs really don't concern me, Mrs Widdowson. Unless you have come to defend yourself against a false accusation——
**Monica** I *have* come for that.
**Rhoda** Indeed?
**Monica** My name has been spoken of in connection with Mr Barfoot.
**Rhoda** (*scornfully*) Spoken of!
**Monica** The man I visited happened to live in the same building as Mr Barfoot. His name is Harry Bevis. There was nothing, nothing whatever, between Mr Barfoot and me.
**Rhoda** Why do you suppose that I should be interested in that?
**Monica** I met him twice after that party we gave, both times by accident. Once at the Royal Academy, and then again in the street. He told me he was going away that day to meet you in Cumberland, or in the hope of meeting you. I understood him to mean that he wished to ask you to—I hoped he might be successful. I have come to you today because I feared you would believe what my husband has accused me of with him.
**Rhoda** Has Mr Barfoot asked you to tell me this?
**Monica** Indeed he has not. If you have any doubt, I can show you the letter which the man I—the man I thought I loved sent me from abroad.

*Pause. Rhoda turns away to hide her feelings. When she turns back, her face is composed*

**Rhoda** I believe you.
**Monica** Oh, Rhoda, what shall I do? How can I go on? I shall not love my child. It will bind me to him for ever.

**Rhoda** Yes, you will love it. That love, that duty, is the life to which you must look forward. How old are you?

**Monica** Twenty-one.

**Rhoda** Well, I am thirty-three, and I don't call myself old. When you have reached my age, I tell you, you will smile at your despair of twelve years ago. If you survive this storm, as you will, you will be all the stronger for it. Don't let yourself be beaten. Above all, stop despising yourself. Say to yourself: this I can do, that I can do, and I will do it.

**Monica** (*takes her hands*) You have such strength.

**Rhoda** You can have as much.

**Monica** How?

**Rhoda** By fighting for something that you believe to be right. You can prove by your life that women can be responsible human beings—trustworthy, and conscious of purpose.

**Monica** How I wish I had come to you before. For your sake too. But now you and Mr Barfoot can——

**Rhoda** No.

**Monica** But——

**Rhoda** No. It is better as it is. Mr Barfoot and I are both too proud. We could not be happy together for long. I would have discovered some things that I shall never know. But I shall achieve more without them.

**Monica** Goodbye, Rhoda. Thank you.

**Rhoda** Goodbye.

*Monica makes to kiss her, but Rhoda turns away*

*Monica goes*

*Rhoda walks around, confused, then sits at her typewriter*


## Scene 11

*Widdowson's house*

*Widdowson alone. A knock at the door*

**Widdowson** Yes?

*Alfred enters*

**Alfred** I beg your pardon, sir.

**Widdowson** I told you I did not wish to be disturbed.

**Alfred** I'm sorry, sir. Miss Madden and Miss Virginia Madden are here. They ask if they may speak with you.

**Widdowson** I did not hear them ring.

**Alfred** They came to the back door.

**Widdowson** Did they indeed? Tell them they may leave by the back door, and that I have nothing to say to them.

**Alfred** With respect, sir, they say it is a matter of the greatest urgency. They seem unusually distressed.

Act II, Scene 11

**Widdowson** I can imagine they do.

*Alfred does not move*

  Well, what are you waiting for? Get rid of them.
**Alfred** Very good, sir.

  *Alfred goes*

*Widdowson stands still for some moments. He takes a cigarette and lights it. He walks up and down. Suddenly, he puts his head in his hands and begins to sob*

**Widdowson** Monica.

*There is a knock at the door*

  (*Shouts*) Must I tell you again? Do you wish to keep your job? Leave me alone.

*The door opens, revealing Alice and Virginia*

  How dare you intrude on me? Get out, the pair of you.
**Alice** We have to speak to you.
**Widdowson** I have nothing to say to you. Get out.
**Virginia** There is something you have to know.

*Widdowson rings the bell*

**Alice** Monica is pregnant and the child is yours.

*Widdowson laughs*

**Virginia** It is true. You are the only man who could be the father.
**Alice** She has proof which she can show you.
**Widdowson** (*laughs*) Proof?
**Virginia** Beyond doubt. She asks if you will take her back. As your wife.

*Widdowson is confused and does not reply at once*

**Widdowson** She has had a lover.
**Alice** She was never his mistress.
**Widdowson** Of course she was.
**Virginia** Only see her and she will prove it to you.

*A knock at the door*

**Widdowson** Yes.

  *Alfred enters*

**Alfred** You rang, sir?

*Pause*

**Widdowson** Leave us.

  *Alfred goes*

**Alice** We promise you, once you have seen her, you will have no doubt.
**Widdowson** I do not——

**Virginia** She only wishes to return to you.
**Widdowson** I do not—wish her to . . . (*He turns his back and stifles a sob*)
*They do not speak*

   Where is she?
**Virginia** At Miss Barfoot's.
**Widdowson** (*suddenly*) You are frightened I will stop your allowance.
**Alice** You have been very generous, Edmund.
**Widdowson** Of going back to live on seven shillings a week.

*Virginia takes Alice's hand*

   (*At length*) Suppose I take her back and the child does not live?
**Alice** She will still be your wife.
**Widdowson** For how long, if there is nothing to bind us? (*Pause*) I will see her when the child is born, and decide then. I promise nothing. Until then, your allowance will continue. Now go. Do not thank me. Go!

*Alice and Virginia leave*

Monica.

## Scene 12

*Mary's house in Chelsea. Some months later*

*Rhoda and Everard*

**Everard** I had to see you again.
**Rhoda** Really? You managed without for several months.
**Everard** I suppose you would never have written to me?
**Rhoda** Never.
**Everard** Because you are too proud, or because the mystery—concerning myself and Mrs Widdowson—is still a mystery?
**Rhoda** There is no longer any mystery.
**Everard** Indeed? You have found what it was all about?
**Rhoda** Yes.
**Everard** Will you tell me?
**Rhoda** No.
**Everard** Why not?
**Rhoda** I don't wish to speak about it.
**Everard** Didn't it occur to you that it would be a kindness to let me know that you no longer suspected me?
**Rhoda** I feel no uneasiness on your account.
**Everard** (*laughs*) Splendidly frank, as ever. You didn't care how much I might suffer?
**Rhoda** You misunderstand me. I felt sure you didn't suffer at all. Otherwise you would have given some sign.
**Everard** (*proud again*) It was not for me to give any sign. (*Pause*) Very well. I admit that an approach was due from me. I have made it. I am here.

Act II, Scene 13

*She does not speak*

So we go back to our day at Wastwater. The perfect day—wasn't it?
**Rhoda** I shall never wish to forget it.
**Everard** And we stand as when we parted that night—do we?
**Rhoda** I think not.
**Everard** Well, now, there's the question we must decide. We must know each other's mind.
**Rhoda** Ah, that is so difficult.
**Everard** Rhoda, let us imagine ourselves back in Cumberland, beside the waves. I repeat what I said then. Rhoda, will you marry me?
**Rhoda** You spoke of "the perfect day". Didn't the day's perfection end before there was any word of marriage? When you put the ring on my finger—it meant you didn't dare risk a free union, because it wasn't equality you wanted.
**Everard** Why do you say that?
**Rhoda** You knew it then and you know it now. In marriage there can never be equality between a man and a woman.
**Everard** Then let us go back to before I spoke of marriage. I loved you, I still love you. Will you live with me in a free union?
**Rhoda** I shall never enter into a marriage or any free union with any man, so we will speak no more of it.
**Everard** In other words you no longer love me?
**Rhoda** (*after a pause*) Yes, I no longer love you. I would have joined you in the free union you seemed to want so much. But the perfection of that day was half make-believe. You wanted to capture me to prove to yourself that I loved you.
**Everard** Perhaps.
**Rhoda** And our living together unmarried was only a fantasy. Oh, Everard, you never loved me entirely. And you will never love any woman—even as much as you loved me.
**Everard** Even now——
**Rhoda** Even now, we can say goodbye as friends. But not if you talk longer. Don't let us spoil it.

*She holds out her hand. He takes it*

**Everard** (*moved*) Your love was worth more than mine. And it will—won't it, Rhoda—be your last? Goodbye.

*Everard goes*

**Rhoda** (*alone*) Goodbye, Everard.

## Scene 13

*The same*

*Alice and Virginia. The doorbell rings*

*Widdowson enters*

**Widdowson** Is it over?
**Alice** At four this afternoon. A little girl.
**Virginia** Monica had to have chloroform.
**Widdowson** And all is well?
**Alice** } (*together*) { I think so.
**Virginia** } { We hope so.
**Alice** The child is pitifully tiny.
**Widdowson** She knows you have sent for me?
**Virginia** Yes. We have something to give you. (*She hands him a sealed envelope*)
**Widdowson** (*looks at the outside*) Please leave me. I wish to read this alone.

*Alice and Virginia go*

*Widdowson opens the envelope and takes out two sheets of paper of different sizes. He looks at one and, after a moment, throws it aside in revulsion. He reads the other half-aloud*

"Dear Edmund, I wish to tell you the truth of my relationship with Bevis. (*He reads silently for some moments. Then*) I tell you all this for the sake of the child that will soon be born. The child is yours, and should not suffer because of what I did. The enclosed letter (*He glances again with revulsion at the sheet he has thrown aside*) will prove this to you if anything can. For myself I ask nothing. If I live, I will consent to anything you propose. I only ask you to behave without pretence. If you cannot forgive me, do not make a show of it. Say what you want and that will be enough". (*He goes to the door. Calls*) Please come in.

*Alice and Virginia enter*

**Widdowson** Take me to her.
**Virginia** Oh, thank you.
**Alice** Thank you.

*He does not reply*

*They take him in to Monica, in bed with the baby in her arms. Alice and Virginia go*

**Monica** Thank you for seeing us, Edmund. I know you did not want to.

*He does not reply*

Look. Here is your daughter.

*She holds the baby towards him. He makes no movement*

Won't you take her?

*Widdowson still makes no movement*

Edmund, she is your child.
**Widdowson** How can I be sure? You have lied to me before. Why not now?
**Monica** Haven't you read Bevis's letter?

Act II, Scene 13

**Widdowson** How do I know that what either of you says is true? That this is not a conspiracy between the two of you. To cover your crime. Do you still love him?
**Monica** No. I did love him, or I thought I did. I wanted to leave you for him and to become his lover.
**Widdowson** His mistress.
**Monica** Yes.
**Widdowson** Why didn't you?
**Monica** He was frightened of the responsibility.
**Widdowson** And of the scandal? (*Contemptuously*) Of losing his good name?
**Monica** Perhaps.
**Widdowson** And you were prepared to abandon me for such a man?
**Monica** Not when I found out what he was like.
**Widdowson** And now you expect me to forget all this and take you back to live with me?
**Monica** For the child's sake.
**Widdowson** Knowing that you do not love me?
**Monica** I have never loved you. I never thought I could.
**Widdowson** Then why did you agree to marry me?
**Monica** Oh, Edmund, you know why. Because I could see no possible future for myself except in marriage. I thought at least that would mean a home, and hopefully children. What else was there for me to do? Spend the rest of my life sitting by the river in the hope that some other man would pick me up like you did?
**Widdowson** You and I can never be happy together. I hate you. And I will hate this child. Always. Even if I come to believe that it is mine, I shall never be able to forget that you conceived it in loathing and disgust. And don't expect me to pay for its upkeep. No court will accept that the thing is mine.

*Pause*

**Monica** Get out of this room. You are beneath contempt. I despise myself for having asked you to be this child's father. You would have treated her even worse than you have treated me. Alice! Virgie!

*They enter*

Show this man the door.

*They stare in alarm*

*Widdowson leaves*

**Alice** Monica, someone else has come to see you.
**Monica** I don't want to see anyone.

*Rhoda enters, with Mary*

**Monica** Hallo, Rhoda. Mary. Oh, Rhoda. I'm frightened. How shall we manage?
**Alice** Don't worry, Monica. Virgie and I will take care of you.
**Monica** How?

**Virginia** We have decided to do what Miss Nunn suggested. We are going to use our little capital to start a school.

**Monica** Oh, Virgie. That's a terrible risk.

**Alice** We shall have to take it. What else have we to live for? Don't worry about us. We shall make it work. We have to, and we can. Don't you think so, Miss Barfoot?

**Mary** Yes. It will be hard, but you know that.

**Rhoda** I believe you will succeed. You two have the same strength as your sister. But you never knew it. Cynics call people like us "odd women", and mock our lives because we shall die unmarried, just as they will mock you, Monica, because your husband has left you and you will bring up your child without a father. How wrong they are. It is women like us who hold the future.

**Monica** (*holds up the baby to Rhoda*) Hold her, Rhoda.

*Rhoda takes the child and stares at it for some seconds. She seems about to break down; controls herself, kisses the child lightly and seems reluctant to let her go. She is still holding her as the Lights fade*

# FURNITURE AND PROPERTY LIST

### ACT I

### Scene 1

*On stage:* Park bench
Book for **Monica**

*Personal:* **Monica:** watch
**Widdowson:** book, card case with card

### Scene 2

*On stage:* Desk. *On it:* primitive typewriter, paper, pen, ashtray, cigarettes, matches
Table. *On it:* teapot, cups, saucers, plate of sandwiches
4 chairs

*Off stage:* Pot of tea **(Mary)**

*Personal:* **Mary:** watch (worn throughout)
**Rhoda:** watch (worn throughout)

### Scene 3

*On stage:* Boat with oars

### Scene 4

*On stage:* Desk. *On it:* primitive typewriter, paper, pen, ashtray, cigarettes, matches
Table
4 chairs

*Personal:* **Everard:** watch

### Scene 5

*On stage:* Boat with oars

### Scene 6

*On stage:* Desk. *On it:* primitive typewriter, paper, pen, ashtray, cigarettes, matches
Table. *On it:* tray with glasses and decanter of sherry
4 chairs

## Scene 7

*On stage:* Table. *On it:* gift-wrapped book
3 chairs

## Scene 8

*On stage:* 2 garden seats
Book for **Rhoda**

## Scene 9

*On stage:* Sideboard. *On it:* buffet supper, glasses, wine
Table. *On it:* ashtray, box of cigarettes, matches
Chairs
Bell pull

# ACT II

## Scene 1

*On stage:* Paintings

*Personal:* **Bevis:** calling card

## Scene 2

*On stage:* Sideboard
Table. *On it:* ashtray, box of cigarettes, matches
Chairs
Bell pull

## Scene 3

*On stage:* Desk. *On it:* primitive typewriter, paper, pen, ashtray, cigarettes, matches
Table. *On it:* **Mary's** purse containing a penny

## Scene 4

*On stage:* Table. *On it:* Pot of tea, jug of milk, cups, saucers, etc., plate of scones, cake
Chairs

## Scene 5

*On stage:* Sideboard
Table. *On it:* ashtray, box of cigarettes, matches
Chairs
Bell pull
Bible

## Scene 6

*Personal:* **Everard:** wedding ring on finger

## Scene 7

*On stage:* Table
Chairs

## Scene 8

*On stage:* Desk. *On it:* primitive typewriter, paper, pen, ashtray, cigarettes, matches
Table
4 chairs

## Scene 9

*Personal:* **Rhoda:** letter

## Scene 10

*On stage:* Desk. *On it:* primitive typewriter, paper, pen, ashtray, cigarettes, matches
Table
4 chairs

## Scene 11

*On stage:* Sideboard
Table. *On it:* ashtray, box of cigarettes, matches
Chairs
Bell pull

## Scene 12

*On stage:* Desk. *On it:* primitive typewriter, paper, pen, ashtray, cigarettes, matches
Table
4 chairs

## Scene 13

*On stage:* Desk. *On it:* primitive typewriter, paper, pen, ashtray, cigarettes, matches
Table
4 chairs
Bed in separate area

*Personal:* **Virginia:** sealed envelope containing 2 sheets of paper

# LIGHTING PLOT

ACT I, SCENE 1. Exterior
*To open:* Bright sunshine effect
*No cues*

ACT I, SCENE 2. Interior
*To open:* Black-out
Cue 1     **Mary** clatters at the typewriter keys            (Page 2)
             *Bring up general lighting*

ACT I, SCENE 3. Exterior
*To open:* Bright sunshine effect
*No cues*

ACT I, SCENE 4. Interior
*To open:* General lighting
*No cues*

ACT I, SCENE 5. Exterior
*To open:* Bright sunshine effect
*No cues*

ACT I, SCENE 6. Interior
*To open:* General lighting
*No cues*

ACT I, SCENE 7. Interior
*To open:* General lighting
*No cues*

ACT I, SCENE 8. Exterior
*To open:* Sunshine effect
*No cues*

# EFFECTS PLOT

## ACT I

| | | |
|---|---|---|
| Cue 1 | The Lights come up for Scene 2<br>*Doorbell* | (Page 2) |
| Cue 2 | **Rhoda:** ". . . if I can help her."<br>*Doorbell* | (Page 4) |
| Cue 3 | **Alice:** "As long as we do not fall ill——"<br>*Doorbell* | (Page 6) |
| Cue 4 | **Rhoda:** "Has he ever married?"<br>*Doorbell* | (Page 12) |
| Cue 5 | To open Scene 6<br>*The doorbell rings* | (Page 17) |
| Cue 6 | **Rhoda:** "But I wish you contentment."<br>*Doorbell* | (Page 18) |
| Cue 7 | **Everard:** "I do."<br>*Clock strikes* | (Page 21) |
| Cue 8 | **Monica:** "Very well."<br>*Doorbell* | (Page 27) |
| Cue 9 | **Widdowson:** "So I put my whole mind to it."<br>*Doorbell* | (Page 28) |
| Cue 10 | **Alfred** offers drinks<br>*Doorbell* | (Page 28) |

## ACT II

| | | |
|---|---|---|
| Cue 11 | To open Scene 2<br>*Front door opens and closes* | (Page 38) |
| Cue 12 | To open Scene 4<br>*Doorbell* | (Page 42) |
| Cue 13 | To open Scene 7<br>*Doorbell* | (Page 47) |
| Cue 14 | **Mary** is typing<br>*Doorbell* | (Page 52) |
| Cue 15 | To open Scene 13<br>*Doorbell* | (Page 59) |

PRINTED IN GREAT BRITAIN BY
THE LONGDUNN PRESS LTD., BRISTOL.